English
Solutions
Book 1

Body rhythm

What is a poem? Why do people lik·
makes someone want to wri·

In this uni·
about p·
what ·

School dinners

How have school meals changed over the years? Are young people at all worried about the effect their diet can have on their health, now and in the future? How can healthy eating encouraged?

·unit you will carry out a survey to see
·abits have changed over the years.
· findings as a repo·

Abc
?&%
1 2 3

English Solutions
Book 1

Jim Sweetman

Shelagh Hubbard

John Mannion

Contents

The activities in this book have been coded by colour, according to the *main* skill used in them. This coding is for ease of reference and does not imply that this skill is the sole focus of the activity: an activity coded a 'reading' activity may involve writing, and a 'speaking & listening' activity may often emerge from a reading activity and lead into a written outcome.

●	=	Speaking & Listening
●	=	Reading
●	=	Writing

Unit title and core activity	Development of key skills	Assignment	Key skills/tips	Cross-curricular options
1. My top ten Discussing, inventing and justifying 'top ten' choices	● Contribute in discussion ● Reach conclusions through discussion ● Write in non-literary ways – giving an opinion	Discussing choices and preferences Reaching agreement in small groups Justifying opinions in writing	Tips: Successful small group discussion; Reaching agreement in small groups Skills: Giving opinions in writing	There are opportunities for links with PSE and RE on personal values
2. How it all began Studying creation stories, including a retelling of Genesis and stories from Australia, Central America, Africa and Scandinavia	● Structure talk for an audience – retelling a story ● Listen carefully and positively ● Engage with content and language – compare creation stories ● Write narrative	Reading and discussing creation stories Storytelling for an audience Writing a creation story	Tips: Presenting stories for a younger audience	Links with RE
3. Body rhythms Exploring an anthology of poems about the body by writers from a range of times and cultures	● Contribute in discussion ● Read poetry ● Write poetry	Reading and discussing poems Analysing techniques in poetry Writing poems	Tips: What is a poem? Writing better poems Skills: The language of poems	
4. A day out Carrying out a range of tasks connected with the organisation of a class outing	● Structure talk for an audience ● Respond and restructure ● Respond to factual and informative texts ● Write in non-literary ways – a formal letter ● Understand and use standard English	Reading timetables and brochures for information Writing a letter to parents Writing and presenting a short talk for peer group pupils	Skills: Writing formal letters	Links to PSE and year group assemblies Links to geography local studies
5. It's a small world Reading extracts from *The Little Man* by Erich Kästner, *Gulliver's Travels* by Jonathan Swift, *The Borrowers Afloat* by Mary Norton, *Truckers* by Terry Pratchett and *The Lord of the Rings* by J R R Tolkien	● Read narrative – including extracts written before 1900 ● Write narrative – empathic stories	Reading and discussing classic literature Writing empathically	Tips: Writing better stories	

Unit title and core activity	Development of key skills	Assignment	Key skills/tips	Cross-curricular options
6. School dinners Studying a magazine article	● Listen carefully and positively – carry out a survey ● Respond to factual and informative texts – magazine articles ● Write in non-literary ways – letters, posters and leaflets	Reading and understanding magazine articles Planning and conducting a survey Writing posters and leaflets	Tips: Survey 'dos and don'ts' Skills: Letters, posters and leaflets; Designing posters and leaflets	Links with `health education and history
7. Dear diary Studying extracts from *Zlata's Diary* by Zlata Filipović and *The Diary of Anne Frank*	● Reach conclusions through discussion ● Respond to factual and informative texts ● Write narrative ● Write in non-literary ways	Writing a letter to Zlata Filipović Writing about a historical event as if you were there Writing a diary	Tips: Effective diary writing	Links with history
8. Early writing Learning about pictograms, hieroglyphics and the development of the modern alphabet	● Understand the development of language ● Engage with content and language ● Write in non-literary ways ● Use presentational devices	Studying and using pictograms		Links with art and design
9. Tomb of the last pharaoh Reading an adventure and completing spoken and written tasks as the story unfolds	● Reach conclusions through discussion ● Respond to factual and informative texts ● Write narrative ● Write in non-literary ways	Writing letters, description, narrative, explanation, script and newspaper article	Skills: Forms of writing – audience and purpose	
10. Turned on its head Comparing extracts from *Maid Marian and her Merry Men* by Tony Robinson and *Bill's New Frock* by Anne Fine	● Engage with content and language ● Read plays ● Write script	Reading and presenting script extracts Analysing comic effects in scripts Writing a script	Tips: Laying out script effectively	
11. Getting into print Exploring the use of print size and layout in a range of texts	● Contribute in discussion ● Respond to factual and informative texts ● Write in non-literary ways ● Use presentational devices	Discussing typeface choices Reading a range of materials and analysing their use of type Writing a poem Designing and writing a newsletter	Tips: Ten things you should remember when starting desk-top publishing	Links with IT, art and design

My top ten

What are the things you really like, and dislike?
What are your favourite things? Special meals? Pop stars and
their music? Bikes? TV programmes? Sports personalities?
What are your 'top ten' favourite things?

> **In this unit you will collect top tens for a display
> and make up some top ten lists of your own. You
> will write about the reasons for your choices and
> discuss how your likes and dislikes change as
> you get older.**

1 Write your own top ten

People have had top tens of favourite things for a long time. An early one was the first pop music Top Ten in the 1950s. Now there are top tens in every magazine and paper that you read. Each one tries to have a top ten that no one else has thought of.

> On this page and the next, there are just a few examples of top tens. Read the first list and then make up your own top ten about one of the things in it. For example, what are *your* top ten nasty vegetables? Which would you put first?

The top ten peculiar top tens

1 Things to eat with cheese
2 Awful pop records
3 Men with beards
4 Worst-dressed teachers
5 Nasty vegetables
6 Naff cars to drive around in
7 Stupid words like 'naff'
8 Worst places to go to with your mum
9 Things that other people think are clever but are actually stupid
10 Worst computer games ever

The top ten things left in taxis

1 Umbrella
2 Mobile phone
3 Bag/suitcase
4 Camera
5 Briefcase
6 Files/Filofax
7 Glasses
8 Package/shopping
9 Wallet/purse
10 Books and jewellery

The top ten people whom Luke Walton (aged 11) will obey

1 My headmaster
2 My teacher
3 My big brother
4 Mum and Dad
5 The police
6 The doctor
7 My dentist
8 The lifeguard at the swimming pool
9 Scout leaders
10 My tennis coach

The top ten things named after their inventors

1	Hoover	*Herbert Hoover*
2	Biro	*Laslo Biro*
3	Sandwich	*John Montagu, Fourth Earl of Sandwich*
4	Zeppelin (a German airship)	*Count Ferdinand von Zeppelin*
5	Wellington boots	*Arthur Wellesley, First Duke of Wellington*
6	Cardigan	*J T Brudnell, Seventh Earl of Cardigan*
7	The Real McCoy	*Benjamin McCoy*
8	Tarmac	*Robert Tarmacadam*
9	Belisha Beacon (pedestrian crossing lights)	*Leslie Hore Belisha*
10	Baker Days (training days for teachers)	*Kenneth Baker*

The top ten reasons for motorway hold-ups

1 Roadworks and contraflows
2 Accidents
3 Motorists looking at an accident on the other side of the motorway
4 Abnormal loads being escorted by the police
5 Sheer weight of traffic
6 HGVs overtaking caravans, going uphill
7 Road surface meltdown in hot weather
8 Rain, sleet, snow, high winds
9 Police patrol car in the inside lane doing 50 mph
10 No apparent reason!

(*AA Magazine*: Issue 6 1993)

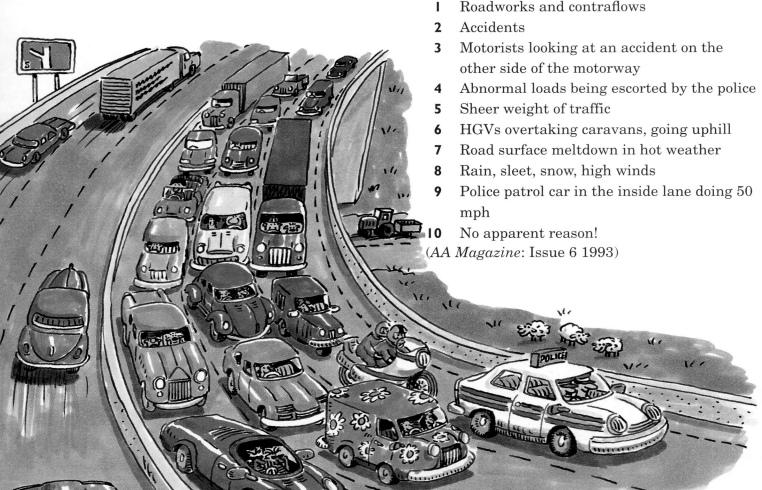

2 Make a class display

Look through newspapers and magazines and collect as many top tens as you can find. A good place to start looking is in music papers, teenage and family magazines and newspaper weekend supplements.

Collect the top tens together for a class display.

3 Discuss in a group

Our likes and dislikes often change as we get older. Your parents, for example, probably don't like what you like. And there are bound to be things they like that you can't stand!

In a group, think about things you used to like, but don't like now. Why did you like them at the time? Why don't you like them now?

Between you, produce a top ten list of things you used to like but don't any longer.

To help you get started, think about:

- toys you had
- food you ate
- places you liked to visit
- programmes you watched on television.

Show your list to the rest of the class.

... on how to make small group discussion a success

 Get ready to talk

Arrange your chairs together round a table.

Appoint one person to note down what people say.

 Take turns

Give all people the space and time to say what they want.

Don't speak when someone else is speaking.

 Ask questions and listen

Ask questions to find out more or just to make things clearer.

Listen carefully to what other people say.

Talk and listen to everyone in the group.

 Bring your ideas together

Give the person who has taken notes a few minutes to organise them.

He or she should then report back to you.

Listen carefully. Suggest additions to the notes if necessary.

4 Write about your choices

It's often easy to say what you like and dislike or how your likes and dislikes have changed. It's much more difficult to say *why* you like or dislike something.

Are there some things *you* like but others don't? Are there other things you hate that everyone else seems to think fantastic?

> Make a list of your current top ten for one of the following:
>
> - Places I would like to visit
> - My favourite music of all time
> - Television programmes (these don't have to be on television at the moment)
> - Books and magazines
> - Films I have seen
> - Computer games I've played
> - Holidays I've been on
> - My favourite clothes.
>
> Now write your list and explain why you chose the top three things on it.

The top five heroic characters at Madame Tussaud's (1992)

1 Superman
2 Marilyn Monroe
3 Arnold Schwarzenegger
4 Winston Churchill
5 Sylvester Stallone

Can you supply numbers 6-10?

The top ten ice cream flavours

1 Vanilla
2 Chocolate
3 Butter pecan
4 Strawberry
5 Neapolitan
6 Chocolate chip
7 French vanilla
8 Cookies and cream
9 Vanilla ripple
10 Praline pecan

The top ten films of Mrs Evans's Year 7 English class

1 Mrs Doubtfire
2 Jurassic Park
3 The Fugitive
4 Hot Shots 2
5 Ace Ventura
6 Dennis
7 Beethoven's 2nd
8 Cool Runnings
9 Aladdin
10 Home Alone

Skills box

Steps to success with your writing

You need to *plan*, *draft*, *revise* and *proof-read* your writing before producing the final version. Follow these steps for success.

1 Plan

Think carefully about your list before you write. Once you start to write, it will be harder to change your mind.

Write down your list. It is probably easiest to list one item under the other.

Think especially hard about your top three choices. You have to explain *why* you chose them. Note down your reasons.

2 Draft

Start with a brief introduction.

Then, use a new paragraph to discuss each of your top three in turn.

Would it be better to start with number one, or to start with number three and write about them in reverse order?

3 Revise

End with a conclusion.

What do you need to sum up? Are your tastes still changing? What do your choices show about you?

Be careful not to repeat yourself. If you use the same word over and over again, your writing will become boring. Try and think of different words for the same thing.

For example, in this piece of writing you might use the words 'choose' and 'because' a lot. Here are some words that you could use instead:

'choose'	'because'
opt for	as
select	on account of
pick	owing to
prefer	since
adopt	in that
decide upon	

4 Proof-read

Check your spelling and punctuation as you write your final version.

5 Present

Show your final draft to your teacher or another pupil.

Here is one final version as an example:

The second place I would like to visit is Eurodisney. I know that some people - like my Dad - think it is a waste of money, but I decided that I really wanted to go after a trip to Alton Towers. Since then, I have had a taste for exciting rides which really scare you, and because Eurodisney has the best rides outside of the United States it has to be among my top choices.

5 Reach an agreement and report back

Another reason why our likes and dislikes change is because people try to change them. Think of the advertisements you see every day on the television, in magazines, along the roads. They are all telling you that you will really like what they are advertising.

Companies spend millions of pounds each year trying to make us like new things. There are advertisements for new kinds of music, new clothes, new sweets, new cosmetics. Many things become fashionable because of the way in which they have been advertised.

> In your group, talk about what is fashionable now that wasn't twelve months ago. Think about:
>
> * new groups, records and dance ideas
> * new films
> * new technologies
> * old ideas that have come back.

The top ten things that never lasted

1 Wham!
2 Eldorado
3 Chopper bikes
4 Sinclair C5s
5 My Little Pony
6 Bell-bottom jeans
7 Shell suits
8 Timeshare holidays
9 Kylie Minogue
10 Ninja Turtles

What can you add to this list?

The top ten things we didn't know we wanted (until they were invented)

1 Hand-held computer games
2 Combined shampoo and conditioner
3 Sports shoes with air bubbles in the soles
4 Alphabet spaghetti
5 Mountain bikes that cover your back with mud
6 Sylvanians
7 Take That
8 Frisbees
9 Trolls
10 Swatch watches

As a group, talk about fashions. Decide which of the reasons below explains best why fashions change.

Agree on a top three in order of importance.

A Advertising persuades us to try out new things.
B Technological inventions are interesting.
C We like to spend our money on something different.
D We like to have the same things as our friends.
E Magazines make new things sound interesting.
F We see new things on television and want them.

Write down your decisions. Report them back to the class.

... on how to agree with one another

 Start off
Each say what you think is most important. Don't interrupt one another.

 Argue your points
You should try to say *why* you hold a particular view. In other words, you have to provide an argument for what you think. Other people may agree or disagree with this argument.
Listen to one another and be ready to change your mind if you find the arguments convincing. Don't be bullied into changing your mind – and don't try to bully others into accepting your arguments!

Make decisions
Once you have finished, you should have decided which of these reasons is the most important. When you have done so, go on to decide about number two on your list.

Report your decision
At the end of the discussion, decide who will report back to the class.

This type of discussion is difficult because you *have* to reach an agreement. That means that you have to listen extra carefully to what others are saying.

6 Make a list of what really matters

What we like and dislike may change as a result of fashion, advertising, where we live, who our friends are, what time we live in. Often our likes and dislikes change as we get older, move to a new school or make new friends.

But there are some things that don't change. These are the things that are *really* important.

Think about some of the things that really matter to you. Family? Friends? World peace? Precious belongings? The environment? Good health? Money? Important memories?

> Make a list. Explain why you included the top five items on it.

on target

After working through this unit, could you:

- give a talk to your class on how things change?

- put a list in order of importance?

- give reasons for your choices?

- take part in a better discussion on another topic?

How it all began

All over the world, there are stories that explain how the world was created. These are called creation stories. These stories have a special importance for many people, because they form part of their religious beliefs. Often, they try to explain the strange and the unexplainable.

In this unit you will read and talk about some of these stories and then perform one of them for the class. You will discuss what the stories have in common and write one of your own.

Reading creation stories

Read these stories about how the Earth was formed.

In the beginning
Elohim the Creator

In the beginning, Elohim, God, created the heavens and the earth. The earth was without form. There was nothing, and darkness was upon the face of the deep. And the Spirit of God was moving over the face of the waters.

And God said, 'Let there be light.'

And there was light. And God saw that the light was good; and God separated the light from the darkness.

God called the light Day, and the darkness He called Night. And there was evening, and there was morning, one day.

And God said, 'Let there be a vault in the midst of the waters, and let it separate the waters from the waters.'

And God made the vault and separated the waters which were under the vault from the waters which were above the vault. And it was so. And God called the vault Heaven. And there was evening, and there was morning, a second day.

And God said, 'Let the waters under the heavens be gathered together into one place. And let the dry land appear.'

And it was so. God called the dry land Earth, and the waters that were gathered together He called Seas. And God saw that it was good.

And God said, 'Let the earth put forth plants yielding seed, and fruit trees bearing fruit in which is their seed, each according to its kind, upon the earth.'

And it was so. The earth brought forth plants yielding seed according to their own kinds, and trees bearing fruit in which is their seed. And God saw that it was good. And there was evening, and there was morning. It was a third day.

And God said, 'Let there be lights in the vault of the heavens to separate the day from the night. And let them be for signs to mark seasons and days and years. And have them shine from the vault of the heavens to give light upon the earth.'

And it was so. And God set the two great lights in the vault of the heavens to separate the light from the darkness. The greater light would rule over the day, and the lesser light would rule over the night. And God saw that it was good. And there was evening, and there was morning, a fourth day.

And God said, 'Let the waters bring forth swarms of living creatures, and let birds fly above the earth across the vault of the heavens.'

And God also created the great sea monsters and every living creature that moves, with which the waters swarm, according to their kinds, and every winged bird according to its kind. And God saw that it was good.

And God blessed them, saying, 'Be fruitful and multiply, and fill the waters in the seas, and let birds multiply on the earth.'

And there was evening, and there was morning. It was a fifth day.

And God said, 'Let the earth bring forth living creatures according to their kinds; cattle and creeping things and beasts of the earth according to their kinds, and the cattle according to theirs. And everything that creeps upon the ground, according to its kind.'

And God saw that it was good.

Then God said, 'Let us make man in our image, after our likeness; and let them have dominion over the fish of the sea, and over the birds of the air, and over the cattle, and over all the earth, and over every creeping thing that creeps upon the earth.'

So God created man in His own image, after our likeness, and He let them have dominion over the fish of the sea, and over the birds of the air, and over the cattle, and over all the earth, and over every creeping thing that creeps upon the earth.

God created man in His own image, in the image of God He created them; male and female He created them. And God blessed them, and God said to them, 'Be fruitful and multiply, and fill the earth and subdue it; and have power over the fish of the sea and over the birds of the air and over every living thing that moves upon the earth.'

And God said, 'Behold, I have given you every plant yielding seed which is upon the face of all the earth, and every tree with seed in its fruit; you shall have them for food.

'And to every beast of the earth, and to every bird of the air, and to everything that has the breath of life, I have given every green plant for food.'

And it was so. And God saw everything that He had made, and behold, it was very good. And there was evening, and there was morning, a sixth day.

Thus the heavens and the earth were finished, and all the host of them. And on the seventh day, God finished His work which He had done, and He rested. So God blessed the seventh day and made it holy. Because on that day, God rested from all His work which He had done in creation.

Virginia Hamilton (from In the Beginning)

The Rainbow Serpent
a creation story from Australia

In the Dreamtime, there were no animals, birds, trees, bushes, hills or mountains. The whole country was flat except for one huge mountain in the North of Australia. At this time, the huge Rainbow Serpent lived on the land. One day he set off to look for his tribe, travelling from the south to the north of Australia. As he travelled, his huge body made deep gorges, and his tracks made rivers and streams. The movement of his long tail made mountains and lagoons. Finally, he found his own people and he hid in secret and watched them as they danced. Then he showed himself to them and was welcomed, as he taught his people new dances, and, from his colours, they found new and lovely colours to wear.

That night there was a storm and everyone took shelter except for two young men who could find no place to shelter. The Rainbow Serpent offered them shelter inside his mouth but then he swallowed them. He knew the people would be angry so he hid at the top of the great mountain. In the morning, the people saw that he was gone. They tracked him to the mountain where he was sleeping. Then, two brave men climbed the peak and, with a knife, cut the young men free from the Rainbow Serpent's belly. The young men turned into parrots the colour of the serpent and flew away.

The next day, when the Rainbow Serpent awoke, he saw that his belly had been cut open and that the men were gone. He was very angry and began to uncoil his tail in a fury. As he moved, the great mountain was thrown apart and where the pieces fell they formed the mountains, hills and valleys of Australia today. The people ran away and turned themselves into animals, birds, insects and plant life so they could hide from the Rainbow Serpent. That is how the land and the plants and the animals were formed. The Rainbow Serpent disappeared forever into the sea but sometimes his eye can be seen by the people as a shooting star that watches them as it travels across the sky.

Frances Halton (from The Creation of the World)

The four creations
a creation story from
Central America

When the world was very new – so new that
only the sky and the sea existed – seven gods
held a council. There were the gods of the
North, South, East and West; Tepeu the
Workman; Gucumatz the Ruler, with his cloak of
green feathers, and Huracan Skyheart.

When they had all settled down, Huracan called
up a great flash of lightning and a growling roll of
thunder. 'Earth!' he cried; and as he spoke the
sea seethed and bubbled, and land formed above
its surface, complete with mountains and valleys
and covered with lush green vegetation.
Gucumatz was delighted.

'What is the point of the Earth if there is no one
to enjoy it?' asked another of the gods. 'Let's
create some perfect beings to live there, who
will worship us and sing our praises.'

So the gods settled down to their new task. First
they created birds, snakes, and wild animals.
'Now worship us and sing our praises,' they
commanded. But the animals had no voices; they
could only whistle, grunt, or bark. The
disappointed gods realised that their first
creations were far from perfect. ' From now on,
you will be hunted, killed, and eaten,' they said
crossly.

The gods decided to try again. They took some
damp earth and shaped it into human beings. But
again they made a mistake; although these beings
could talk, when the earth dried they were so
solid that they could not turn their heads, but
looked straight in front – and what was more
serious, they dissolved if they got wet! Worst of

all, the gods had given them no intelligence.
Angrily, they destroyed their creations and
thought again. 'Let's try wood,' they said.

Soon Earth was filled with wooden people. They
talked, they had children, they built houses – but
they had no feelings. They never thought about
their creators. The disappointed gods drove
them from the Earth. Only a very few managed
to hide themselves in the forests, where they
gave birth to little tree-dwelling monkeys.

The gods were determined to create their
perfect people, cost what it might. They called
another council. 'We must find a truly noble
substance with which to form the flesh and

blood of these people – something which will also give them life, strength and intelligence,' they said. 'But where can we find such a thing?'

As they puzzled, four animals came to find them; the wild cat, the coyote, the parakeet, and the kite. 'We know where you can find just what you want,' they said. 'Follow us!'

They led the gods to a field where yellow and white maize was growing.

'Here are the magic plants from which we can make our people!' exclaimed the gods. They plucked the corncobs, ground the white and yellow grains to flour, and made a paste from which they formed four people. At last they had succeeded. These people thanked their creators and sang their praises. They became as intelligent as the gods themselves, and they could even see in the dark. The gods were uneasy. 'We have done our work too well,' they said to one another. 'We must check their powers.' So the gods threw mist over the eyes of the people, which dimmed their sight until they could only see things close to them. Then the gods were satisfied at last.

Frances Halton (from *The Creation of the World*)

Muluku and the monkey men
a creation story from Africa

The great god Muluku dug two holes in the
Earth, and pulled out two living creatures.
They stood upright on their hind legs, and
looked at him as if waiting for orders.

'Here are Man and Woman!' cried Muluku
happily. He thought that he had given life to
intelligent creatures and he decided to give them
a test. 'Listen carefully,' he said. 'Here is a pick;
till the soil with it, then sow some millet from
this bag. With this axe, cut down branches and
build a shelter. When you are hungry, cook
some millet in this pot. I will leave you burning
logs for a fire; don't let it die out!' And Muluku,
who had other things to attend to, soared away
from Earth.

Some time later, Muluku came back to see how
his people were getting on. But where was the
hut he had told them to build? The cooking pot
lay broken beside the ashes of their fire, and
nearby lay the empty millet bag and the pick. At
last Muluku found the people in the forest; they
had decided not to work, but to live like the
animals.

Muluku flew into a rage. Calling two apes, he
gave them the same tools and the same orders.
The two animals did just as he had asked.
So Muluku said to them: 'From now on, you shall
be human beings!' Then he seized the man and
the woman, and said sternly: 'Now you are
monkeys; that is all you are worth.'

Frances Halton (from *The Creation of the World*)

In a small group, talk about the Rainbow Serpent, the Four Creations and Muluku and the Monkey Men.

Have you heard or read similar stories from other places?

Do the three stories have any points in common? Think about your answers to these questions:

a What does each story explain about the way things are?

b How do the gods behave in each story?

c Where does fate or chance play a part?

d How would you describe the language used to tell the stories?

2 Retell a creation story

Work as a group to present one of the stories for an infant school audience.

You could:

- retell the story using a number of voices

- dramatise it

- use mime and a narrator

- add sound effects and music.

Remember that you have to tell the story simply so that a younger audience will understand it.

Plan and rehearse your presentation, then perform it for the class.

... on how to perform stories for a younger audience

1 Remember that the audience may not be able to concentrate for long

You need to keep the children's interest by entertaining them.

So, the performance will have to be *fast moving, lively* and *colourful.* If possible, the audience should be able to join in. It should not go on too long.

2 The audience may not know as many words as you

Younger children could have difficulty with the characters' names.

The performance will have to use easy words. It will also help if you choose pupils who *look* very different to take the part of the different characters.

The story will have to be told in clear, simple language.

3 Look in detail at a creation story

Read the story below by Geraldine McCaughrean. It is called *The cow and the giant*. It retells a Viking creation story. The Vikings were known to be a violent, warlike race. They are no different in this story!

The cow and the giant

At the centre of the world was a hole, a pit, a nothingness: Ginnungagap. To the north were icy fogs and streams of poisonous cold, and to the south, fields of fire. The freezing streams spilled over the brink of Ginnungagap and filled it with glaciers of poisonous ice. Ice and fire. Fire and ice. For aeons they clashed, like sword on shield, like flint on flint, until the sparks flew up one day over the brink of Ginnungagap and took shape where they landed.

And what shapes they took! A huge man and a huger cow, with only each other for company. Ymir the Giant lay beneath the cow each day and milked her, squirting the white milk directly into his cavernous mouth. When he was not drinking, he slept, a creature so ugly that even the cow rarely turned her head in his direction.

While Ymir drank and slept, the cow licked the salty, ice-slippery rim of Ginnungagap, staring down into the depths with doleful, brown eyes. Her great tongue rasped over the stones until, after a million years or so, the stones were quite worn down. One day, while Ymir lay snoring, the cow's tongue licked something hairy and warm –

the curly top of a man's head. Soon she had laid bare face and chest, arms and legs, and up sprang Buri as if woken by the licking of his dog. He was as handsome as Ymir was ugly, and smaller, too – more like you and me. He crossed to where the sleeping giant lay milky-mouthed beneath the cow.

Ymir did not wake but all of a sudden his body began to stir. From out of his hairy ears, his flaring nostrils, his lolling mouth, his armpits crept gruesome little children who grew, instantly, into a brotherhood of ice-giants. Their heads were stone, their shoulders like boulders, their hands and feet carved from ice and their beards were needles of frost. Some changed into eagles and swooped about the sunless, moonless Overhead. Some howled themselves into wolves. But the rest snarled and sneered about them, hunched and punching, ready for a fight. They kicked the cosmic cow and smashed the ice with their fists. They hurled icicle daggers into Ginnungagap just to hear the echo. They were foul-mouthed and rough, swaggering and crude, and their breath froze in the air like bird-droppings. Last of all, from under the arches of Ymir's feet emerged a hideous six-headed troll.

'I'd like a son,' thought Buri, 'but not like any of these.' Just then, from out of Ymir's cupped and sleeping hands, and from under his eyelids came female giants – more attractive than the males by far, with their rain-dark hair and snow-white skin. Indeed, one was so fair that Buri took note of her name – Bestla – and married her. From this handsome couple came the first gods.

But the children of Ymir – the ice-giants – grew up unruly and coarse, throwing insults and punches and rocks all day long. War soon broke out between the sons of Buri and Bestla and the sons of Ymir. The ice-giants used the sleeping Ymir as their citadel, crouching behind his legs, catapulting ice-blocks over his nose, leaping on his spongy stomach to shout oaths at their enemy. The gods stormed their citadel, scaling Ymir's arms, setting fire to his hair. Finally they opened a wound so deep that the blood leapt out like water through a breached dam. It sluiced away whole ranks of ice-giants; swept them quite away. It washed away the camp where the womenfolk sat cooking, and drowned their stone-headed, hooligan children. Only one ice giant, Bergelmir, escaped with his wife, jumping into a hollow tree-trunk and floating away over rapids of foaming blood in the world's very first canoe.

Then, the sons of Buri took hold of Ymir's feet and dragged the body to the brink of Ginnungagap's yawning chasm. Perhaps they intended to roll it over into the poisonous ice pit below. But as they dragged him along, they noticed how his spilt blood puddled and pooled into lakes and tarns of fresh water. Alive, Ymir had done nothing but drink and sleep; maybe dead he could be of more use.

So out of his flesh the triumphant gods made soil – a layer deep enough to cover the flat, icy ground. From his bones they made mountains. From the unburned locks of his hair they made trees curly with leaves, tendrilled vines and beans. Heaving his massive skull into the air, they appointed four dwarfs – Northman, Southman, Eastman and Westerman – to hold it up high for ever. When they slung Ymir's brains upwards,

too, they tattered into clouds and drifted about without falling back to Earth.

It was hard to see their finished handiwork in the dark, so the gods travelled south to the Land of Fire. There they captured, like leaping salmon, sparks enough to make sun, moon and stars. And they lit the place they had made, and called it 'Midgard' or 'Middle Earth', because it stood between the lands of Fire and Ice.

Geraldine McCaughrean (from On the Day the World Began)

Write your answers to these questions:

a How does the story explain the creation of:

- eagles and wolves
- lakes and tarns
- soil
- mountains
- clouds
- sun, moon and the stars?

b What impression does the story give of this world during its creation? Why do you think it is described in this way?

c Describe two places where the story creates a powerful picture in words for the listener. What makes them effective?

4 Write your own creation story

Use all that you have read to help you write your own creation story.
Write a story which can be read aloud to younger children.

Follow these steps for success:

1 Decide on an idea for your story
To help you get started, think about features of the Earth, like mountains, rivers and seas. Think about how your story can 'explain' how these were created. What part might a God, or Gods, have played in this creation?
Note down your ideas as you plan your story.

2 Use your notes to draft the basic story you intend to tell
Think about any characters involved: remember that humans are often not the most important part of creation stories! How will you build up interest in your story?

3 Discuss your draft version with a partner
Share ideas and listen carefully to comments. Your partner may have suggestions for making your story more interesting, and you should change your plan if necessary.

4 Be prepared to write a second draft
You won't always need to do this, but this is a good way of including all the points you and your partner have thought about. The story will probably be much better as a result.
If you don't write a second draft, proof-read the original, checking for spelling and punctuation errors.

5 Write your final version
You are going to read this story aloud, so keep the language simple and the sentences short. Use direct speech (the words characters actually say) and powerful description.

6 **Read your finished creation story aloud to the class**
Your story is important! Make sure that your reading is clear, expressive and loud enough to do justice to it.

on target

After working through this unit, could you:

● retell a creation story well?

● describe some of the features of a creation story?

● capture the style and form of a creation story in your own version?

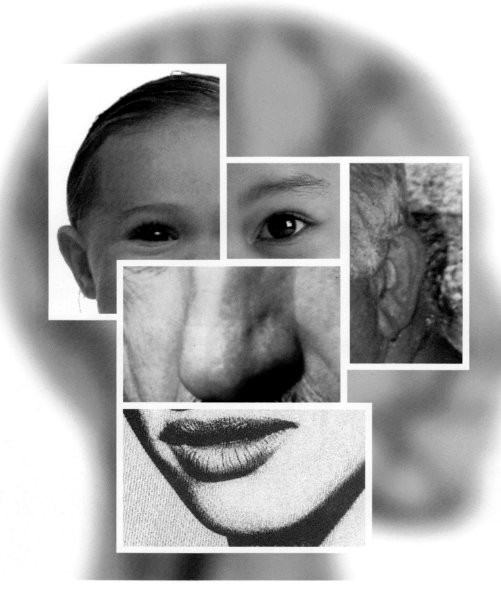

Body rhythms

What is a poem? Why do people like to read poetry? What makes someone want to write a poem?

In this unit you will read and write some poetry about parts of the body. You will learn about what poems are and how they work.

Look at faces

With a partner, study the faces on this page.

They say that every picture tells a story. What stories do these pictures tell you about the people they show?

Pick one of the faces. Write a description of what you can see and what that makes you think about the person. Write in draft form or make notes.

2 Reading poems

The poems on these pages have one thing in common. They are all about parts of the body.

Often, the poet isn't only interested in saying what the part of the body looks like. In many of these poems, the poet uses physical description of the body as a way of going on to talk about something else.

Read the poems.

My dad

I love to watch my dad
when he's cutting his toenails.
My dad does not mind
if he has an audience.
He is like a medical TV show
during a tricky operation.
He says, 'First you trim the nail
leaving a strip of white at the top
before probing under the nail for crud.'
The crud is all different colours
because it is fluff from his socks.
He cannot understand people
who think that's all there is
to cutting your nails.
Neither can I.
Next he wedges a tiny pair of silver scissors
into the corner and takes another scissors
and goes clip, clip, clip.
That's for ingrown toenails.
To polish things off,
he scrapes the sides of his nail
with a little file just in case.
I would like to be skilled
as my dad at cutting toenails
in the years to come.

Julie O'Callaghan

Haircut

I said, I want it short,
Short back and sides.
I told him, man, I told him,
When I took him aside,
I said I want a haircut
I can wear with pride,
So leave it long on top
But short back and side.
I said, try and put a pattern
In the shorter part,
You could put a skull and crossbones
Or an arrow through a heart,
Be sure I have enough hair left
To cover my wart,
Leave a little on the top
But the rest – keep it short.
Well, boy, he started cutting
And I settled down to wait,
He was cutting from seven
Till half-past-eight,
I started getting worried
When I saw that it was late
But then he put the scissors down
Said, 'there you are, mate.'

Well, I did see a skull and a
criss-cross bone or two,
They were my own skull and bones
That were peeping through
I looked just like a monkey
That I saw once at the zoo,
He said, 'What's the matter, Tammy,
Don't you like the hair-do?'
Well, I felt my heart stop beating
When I looked at my reflection,
I felt like something frizzled out
Right in my middle section,
I looked around for somewhere
I could crawl into and hide,
The day I let my brother cut
My hair short back and sides.

Valerie Bloom

Heart

I wake at three, in some slight pain.
I hear no sound of clock or rain,
No chorus of the stars, no gong,
Mosquito, siren, horn or plane.

Only my heart beats slow and strong,
I listen to its certain song,
It does not sympathise but strives,
To beat all night and all day long.

Whether my spirit soars or dives,
My blood, at its compulsion, drives,
Through its elastic chambers, through
My arteries, my veins, my lives.

Above all, to my heart I'm true.
It does not tell me what to do.
It beats, I live, it beats again.
For what? I wish I knew it knew.

Vikram Seth

Valentine

My heart has made its mind up
And I'm afraid it's you.
Whatever you've got lined up,
My heart has made its mind up
And if you can't be signed up
This year, next year will do.
My heart has made its mind up
And I'm afraid it's you.

Wendy Cope

A girl's head

In it there is a dream
that was started
before she was born,

and there is a globe
with hemispheres
which shall be happy.

There is her own spacecraft,
a chosen dress
and pictures of her friends.

There are shining combs
and a maze of mirrors.

There is a diary
for surprise occasions.

There is a horse springing hooves
across the sky.

There is a sky that
tides and swells
and cannot be mapped.

There is untold hope
in that no equation exactly
fits a head.

Katherine Gallagher

A boy's head

In it there is a space-ship
and a project
for doing away with piano lessons.

And there is
Noah's ark, which shall be first.

And there is
an entirely new bird,
an entirely new hare,
an entirely new bumble-bee.

There is a river
that flows upwards.

There is a multiplication table.

There is anti-matter.

And it just cannot be trimmed.

I believe
that only what cannot be trimmed
is a head.
There is much promise
in the circumstance
that so many people have heads.

Miroslav Holub

36

Upon shaving off one's beard

The scissors cut the long-grown hair;
The razor scrapes the remnant fuzz.
Small-jawed, weak-chinned, big-eyed I stare
At the forgotten boy I was.

John Updike

The village blacksmith

Under a spreading chestnut-tree
The village smithy stands;
The smith, a mighty man is he,
With large and sinewy hands;
And the muscles of his brawny arms
Are strong as iron bands.

His hair is crisp, and black, and long,
His face is like the tan;
His brow is wet with honest sweat,
He earns whate'er he can,
He looks the whole world in the face,
For he owes not any man.

Henry Wadsworth Longfellow

Upon her feet

Her pretty feet
Like snails did creep
A little out, and then,
As if they started at bo-peep,
Did soon draw in again.

Robert Herrick

On Julia's legs

Fain would I kiss my Julia's dainty leg,
Which is as white and hairless as an egg.

Robert Herrick

Body rhythms

Her belly

She has a right to have a fat belly,
her belly has borne five children.
They warmed themselves at it,
it was the sun of their childhood.

The five children have gone,
her fat belly remains.
This belly
is beautiful.

Anna Swirsczynska

Phizzog

This face you got,
This here phizzog you carry around,
You never picked it out for yourself, at all, at all
   – did you?
This here phizzog – somebody handed it to you
   – am I right?
Somebody said, 'Here's yours, now go see what
   you can do with it.'
Somebody slipped it to you and it was like a
   package marked:
'No goods exchanged after being taken away' –
   This face you got.

Carl Sandburg

Wheels-song

I don't know why I've got feet
when I could have had wheels,
for wheels go so much faster.

Imagine people turning to stare,
and all telling me to slow down
before I caused a disaster.

Imagine me gliding off into space
with a brief sure nod to the Moon,
then simply going straight past her.

Imagine ...

Katherine Gallagher

I don't cry

Throat burns,
Eyes sting,
Face swells,
Reddening.

Nose sniffs,
Lips quake,
Chin trembles,
Legs shake.

Tears drop.

You what?
Crying?
Me! Cry!
Nah – I've just got something in my eye ...

Michaela Morgan

Pick two of the poems and talk to a partner about them. Try to say:

- what you liked about them
- what you think they are about
- why you chose them.

Sometimes these poems will say more about a person than just what he or she looks like. Can you describe how the poems you have picked do this?

3 What is a poem?

Look at these lines with a partner.

> Decide between you which of them are
> poetic and which – if any – are not. Jot
> down your reasons.
>
> Join another pair and see how far you
> agree. Share your conclusions with the
> class.

A

Police are searching for a middle-aged man
with a round face,
dark hair and glasses.

B

Tiny fingers, tiny toes
Turned up feet and a turned up nose.

C

The winter evening settles down
With smells of steaks in passageways.
Six o'clock.

D

My beard used to be brown, but now it's grey
And turning white with every day

E

A shoulder of rock
Sticks up out of the sea,
A fisherman's mark
For lobster and blue-shark.

F

Grey-muzzled, granddad lumbers
like an old elephant to water
in the dry season.
Only the penetrating sapphires in his eyes
Reveal the senses which lead him.

G

My beard is grey but I live a colourful life.

H

Then a soldier,
Full of strange oaths,
and bearded like the pard,
Jealous in honour, sudden and quick in quarrel
Seeking the bubble reputation
Even in the cannon's mouth.

I

When I do count the clock that tells the time,
I see the brave day sunk in hideous night;
When I behold the violet past prime,
And sable curls all silvered o'er with white;
When lofty trees I see barren of leaves,
Which erst from heat did canopy the herd,
And summer's green all girded up in sheaves,
Borne on the bier with white and bristly beard.

(On page 45 you will find which of these form
part of a poem and which do not.)

Tips ...

... on what makes a poem

Experts and writers have always disagreed over exactly what a poem is.

However, people have defined poetry as the use of words which:

● are given extra meaning by the way in which they are arranged

● use rhyme for effect

● use rhythm for effect

● use old-fashioned language

● use words in new and unfamiliar ways

● make interesting associations or unusual comparisions

● are lively and unpredictable

● are used to create sounds

● create pictures

● give objects life.

4 Look at people

Think of a person you know well. It could be a friend, a relative or a more famous personality. What is it about this person that sums up what he or she is like? Is it:

● what he or she looks like

● the kind of things he or she says

● the things he or she does (his or her mannerisms)?

Write the first draft of a poem about this person. Use the notes you have made to form a picture of him or her.

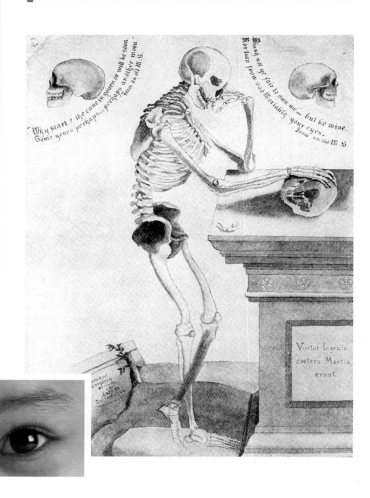

5 Write your own poem

Write your own poem about a part of the body.

Use your earlier drafts or start again from scratch. As you write, remember that the body can be a starting point for thinking and talking about other subjects.

Read your poem with the class. Display neat copies of the poems on a giant cut-out of a human body – or a human skeleton, as here, if you feel particuarly gruesome!

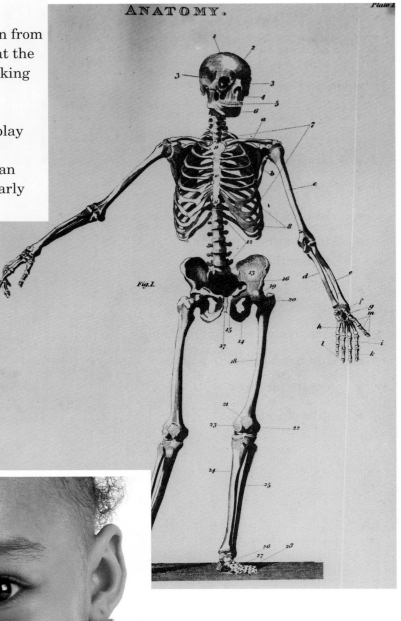

Skills Box

The language of poems

1 Making comparisons

There are two basic forms of comparison – *similes* and *metaphors*.

A *simile* is a comparison which compares one thing with something else. You can recognise a simile by the use of the words 'like' or 'as':

My face is like a greasy ball, my spots are like volcanoes.

A *metaphor* is a comparison where something is described as if it really *is* the thing it is being compared to:

My spots are volcanoes erupting on my cratered face.

An *extended simile* or *metaphor* continues the comparison.

Here is an *extended simile*:

Like a new volcano my spots erupt a yellow lava.

Here is an *extended metaphor*:

My spots are volcanoes spurting yellow rocks from a flaming cone of pain.

2 Using sound patterns

Sounds are created in poems in three ways: *alliteration, assonance, onomatopoeia*. These often overlap in use.

Alliteration is where the sound of the first letter of each word is repeated, for example:

My spots spurt stinking slime across my face.

Assonance is where the sound of the words is repeated, for example:

My fingers sliver slippery on the surface of slime

Onomatopoeia is where the sound of a word reflects its meaning (like 'BANG'), for example:

Squelch, squash, pop, splurt, You only feel better if it hurts!

... on how to write better poems

1. Get words down on paper
Think, and talk, about the subject. Scribble down words and ideas without putting them in order. (This is often called 'brainstorming'.)

2. Write in silence
Concentrate on the words you're writing.

3. Plan, draft and redraft until you get it right

4. Keep your drafts
Even if you are using a word processor, you may want to go back to them and combine them.

5. Choose words carefully
Your words should describe your ideas as accurately as possible.

6. Add, or extend, comparisons as you redraft

7. Bring out the sound patterns in your words

8. Don't use rhyme for the sake of it
If your poem is going to rhyme, find the best word with the right meaning. Don't just include words because they rhyme.

9. Think carefully about the rhythm of your poem
Make the rhythm of the words reflect the feelings you want to produce. Short words give a feeling of excitement, longer ones give a relaxed or thoughtful tone.

10. Produce a neat final version
Check you have chosen the best place to break the lines as you set the poem out on the page.

on target ?

After working through this unit, could you:

- write a better poem on a different subject of your choice?

- describe to a friend what poetry is?

- give your own examples of similes, metaphors and sound patterning?

Answers to Activity 3 (What is a poem?, on page 40)
C, E, H and I were taken from poems. The other pieces were invented.

A day out

Planning a day out for yourself can be fun. When it is for a school party, good organisation is crucial to the success of the day.

 In this unit you will read various pieces of information, including bus and rail timetables, a map and descriptions of places to visit. You will then plan a class outing.

I The background

For this unit, imagine that you are a pupil at a secondary school in Farwood. The theatre in Blackton is putting on a play you are studying, and your English teacher has booked tickets for your class of 20 pupils for the 4.00 pm performance. The headteacher has suggested you make a day out of the occasion and has asked your group to make the arrangements.

The only restrictions are:

- you cannot leave before 8.20 am
- you must arrive back before 9.00 pm
- the pupils should do a number of things, at least two of which should have something to do with work they are doing at school
- you must use the local £4.00 Rover ticket, which allows you to use the bus and rail services for as many journeys as you want for 24 hours.

Two other things to bear in mind are that:

- the School Fund can give £2 to any pupil who needs help with money
- you could arrange to take packed lunches.

2 Make plans for the day

Use the information on these pages to help you plan your day.

While you are deciding how to spend your time, remember to bear in mind:

- how much your arrangements will cost
- where to have lunch
- what you will do if it rains.

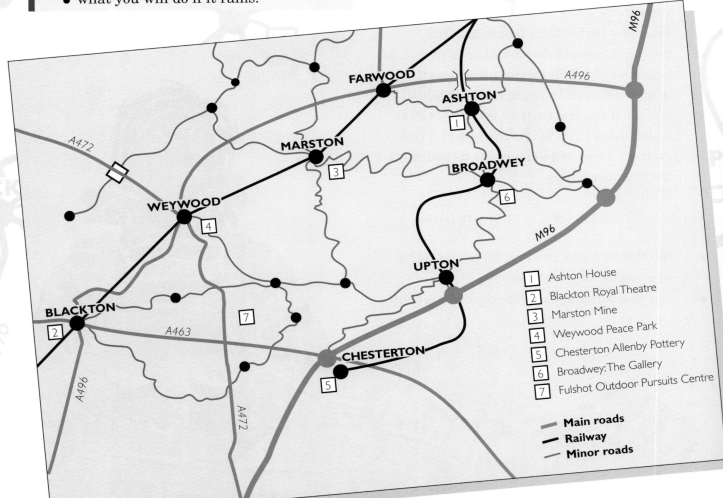

1 Ashton House
2 Blackton Royal Theatre
3 Marston Mine
4 Weywood Peace Park
5 Chesterton Allenby Pottery
6 Broadwey: The Gallery
7 Fulshot Outdoor Pursuits Centre

Main roads
Railway
Minor roads

Bus timetables

Route			
Farwood – Ashton	0805 0820	0830 0850	0855 0915
Ashton – Farwood	0825 0845	0855 0915	0920 0940
Ashton – Marston	0840 0910	0900 0930	0930 1000
Marston – Ashton	0910 0940	0930 1000	1000 1030
Marston – Broadwey	0900 0940	1100 1140	1300 1340
Broadwey – Marston	0800 0840	1000 1040	1200 1240
Marston* – Upton	0920 1000	0940 1020	1000 1040
Upton* – Marston	1000 1040	1020 1100	1040 1120
Upton – Blackton	0900 1000	1000 1100	1100 1200
Blackton – Upton	1000 1100	1100 1200	1200 1300
Upton – Chesterton	0805 0820	0820 0835	0835 0850
Chesterton – Upton	0815 0830	0830 0845	0845 0900
Weywood – Chesterton	0730 0830	0840 0940	1000 1100
Chesterton – Weywood	0830 0930	0940 1040	1100 1200
Chesterton – Blackton	0710 0730	0720 0740	0800 0820
Blackton – Chesterton	0730 0750	0740 0800	0820 0840

* Bus stops at Outdoor Pursuits Centre
(20 minutes from either direction)

Train timetables

Farwood	0800	0825	0840	0900	0935	0940 …	and at the same minutes past each hour
Marston	0810	0835	0850	0910	0935	0950 …	
Weywood	0830	0855	0910	0930	0955	1010 …	
Blackton	0900	0925	0940	1000	1025	1040 …	

Blackton	1605	1730	1845	1930 …	and at the same minutes past each hour
Weywood	1635	1800	1915	2000 …	
Marston	1655	–	1935	– …	
Farwood	1705	1820	1945	2020 …	

Ashton	0815	0845	0900 …	and at the same minutes past each hour
Broadwey	0845	0915	– …	
Upton	0900	0930	– …	
Chesterton	0930	1000	1010 …	

Chesterton	1540	1610	1630 …	and at the same minutes past each hour
Upton	1610	1640	– …	
Broadwey	1625	1655	– …	
Ashton	1655	1725	1740 …	

Possible places to visit

Ashton House

Entry fee: £1.75p. Built in 1580 to the design of the famous navy captain, Henry Ashton, later Lord Ashton, this houses many fascinating exhibits relating to the history of the British at sea. Many of the fortifications, built to withstand the Roundheads during the Civil War, still remain. A guided tour is available, lasting about 45 minutes.

Blackton Royal Theatre

Tickets for groups of 20 or more: £5.00 each. The theatre is a fine piece of Georgian architecture and has recently been refurbished. It is enjoying a period of great critical acclaim. There is currently an exhibition in the foyer, borrowed from the Royal Shakespeare Company, entitled *Changing Faces*. This focuses on how various actors have interpreted the great roles of Shakespeare. The paintings, drawings, photographs and posters range from the early seventeenth century to the present day.

Marston Mine

Entry fee: £3.50. One of the first to open and the last to close, Marston Mine has been preserved to give a sense of what life in a deep mine used to be like. One of the unforgettable moments occurs when visitors find themselves a mile underground and then the lights are switched off! A museum on the surface traces the rise and fall of an important local industry. Trips down the mine take about 25 minutes and run every 30 minutes from 9.30 to 4.30.

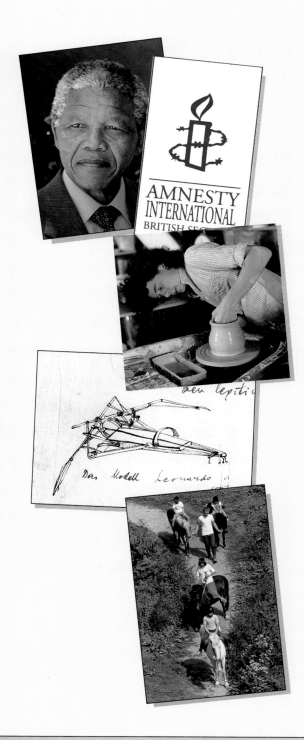

Weywood Peace Park

Entry: free. Opened in 1990 by Nelson Mandela, this park is devoted to the memory of all those who have sought peace in the world. Those commemorated include Gandhi, Martin Luther King and Alfred Nobel, and there is a recently-opened section devoted to Amnesty International. The exhibition hall focuses on the lives of all those who are celebrated in the park. The gardens themselves have won many awards for floral design.

Chesterton Allenby Pottery

Entry fee: £1.50p. This guided tour of the factory, lasting about an hour, allows you to watch skilled potters and artists working with traditional techniques. Those who wish to can also participate in the making of a vase or plate.

Broadwey: the Gallery

Entry: free. An exhibition of the drawings of Leonardo da Vinci will be the centre point of this season's showing. One room of special interest focuses on da Vinci's inventions, including his famous designs for a flying machine.

Fulshot Outdoor Pursuits Centre

Entry fee: £3.00. Only recently opened, this has already become one of the most popular places to visit in the area. Activities include clay pigeon shooting, archery, sailing, swimming, climbing, graded assault courses and a short course on first aid. For younger people, there are also pony rides, a go-kart course and a chance to try out the newest scrambling bikes. Most activities are available in 30-minute or one-hour slots.

3 Decide where to go

Use a grid like the one below to work out which places you could visit. It may be a good idea to prepare several alternative grids to help you with the timing and costs of the day out.

Think carefully about the amount of time each visit will take. Don't forget that people aren't always on time and may need to be rounded up! You will need to add in some time for this.

4 Explain your choice

Your teacher will want to know what you have chosen for your class's day out. He or she will need to be sure that you are not planning to waste the school's money, or your fellow pupils' time!

Prepare a short talk which will explain which places you are planning to visit and why you have decided to go there. Be prepared for your teacher to ask you about the cost of the arrangements and the timing of your programme.

Give your talk to your teacher, the class, or to a small group of pupils.

Day planner

Places of interest	Times for visit	Total time	Arrival and departure time		Costs
Marston Mine	25 minutes in mine	1 hour	a. 9.10	d. 10.35	£3.50
Weywood Peace Park	35 minutes to look round				

When you know what is possible, you can decide which set of activities will make the most interesting day.

5 Write a letter to the parents

Now that you have decided where to go, you must tell parents what you are planning.

Write a letter giving the details of the day out.

In your letter, give reasons why you will be visiting the places you have chosen. Include a timetable for the day and remind parents that help with the cost is available.

At this stage, you need to think about:

- the style of the letter
- any other information which parents will require
- whether you should mention that pupils will have worksheets to complete
- if you will use a tear-off slip or a separate form for the reply
- how soon you would like an answer to the letter.

You might like to read the Skills box on writing formal letters (pages 54–55), before you tackle this exercise.

6 Prepare a talk for the pupils

The day for the outing arrives. Now, prepare a talk to the group in which you will give some advice about the trip.

You will need to include all the details for the day's events: the times, the places where pupils will be picked up and dropped off and any other relevant details. Be prepared to answer questions. Think about:

- organising what you have to say so it can be clearly understood
- being concise (short and to the point)
- reminding pupils how they should behave, in the theatre and elsewhere.

Present your talk to the class.

Skills box

Writing formal letters

There are a number of conventions (or rules) about writing and setting out formal letters. These vary slightly depending on how formal the letter is and whether it is handwritten or typed.

Addressing and dating your formal letter

You either punctuate all your address:

15, Cornwallis Terrace,
Clifton,
Bristol,
Avon,
BS8 7ET.

or you leave it unpunctuated:

15 Cornwallis Terrace
Clifton
Bristol
Avon
BS8 7ET

You should normally give the date of writing below your address. There are a number of ways of doing this:

11 August 1999
11/8/99
11–8–99
11th August 1999

Greetings and farewells in formal letters

If you know the person you are writing to, you address him or her by name:

Dear Mrs Chubb
Dear Ms Kandola

If you do not know the person you are writing to, you address him or her by title:

Dear Editor
Dear Personnel Manager
Grimm Computers Ltd
Dear Year 7 Parent

If you know the sex of the person you are writing to, but you still do not know the person's name:

Dear Sir or
Dear Madam

In all other cases, use:

Dear Sir/Madam

If you are signing off a letter to a named person (one that you have started, for example, 'Dear Mrs Chubb'), then you write:

Yours sincerely

If you are signing off a letter to an unnamed person (one that you have started, for example, 'Dear Sir' or 'Dear Parent'), then you write:

Yours faithfully

Formal letters also often include the following:

The name and address of the person you are writing to – punctuated like your address

A reference

A heading to describe the subject of the letter

Subheadings for clarity

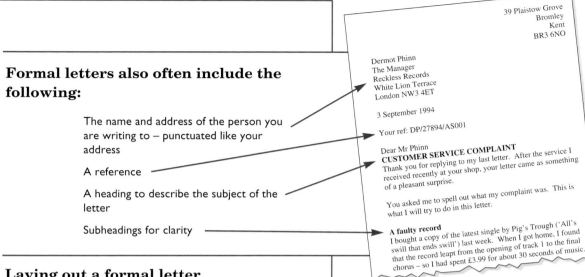

> 39 Plaistow Grove
> Bromley
> Kent
> BR3 6NO
>
> Dermot Phinn
> The Manager
> Reckless Records
> White Lion Terrace
> London NW3 4ET
>
> 3 September 1994
>
> Your ref: DP/27894/AS001
>
> Dear Mr Phinn
> **CUSTOMER SERVICE COMPLAINT**
> Thank you for replying to my last letter. After the service I received recently at your shop, your letter came as something of a pleasant surprise.
>
> You asked me to spell out what my complaint was. This is what I will try to do in this letter.
>
> **A faulty record**
> I bought a copy of the latest single by Pig's Trough ('All's swill that ends swill') last week. When I got home, I found that the record leapt from the opening of track 1 to the final chorus – so I had spent £3.99 for about 30 seconds of music.

Laying out a formal letter

Here are three ways to lay out a formal letter. Whichever style you choose, make sure you keep to it throughout the letter!

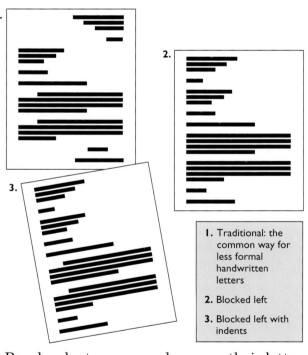

1. Traditional: the common way for less formal handwritten letters

2. Blocked left

3. Blocked left with indents

People who type or word-process their letters usually use one of these types now.

on target ?

After working through this unit, could you:

● be confident that your day – timings and prices – would work out as you planned?

● say what are the important things to bear in mind when writing to parents?

● speak to the group confidently and informatively?

It's a small world

Ever since people started telling stories, there have been
tales about the little people who share our world. There are
stories of fairies, elves, leprechauns and other small people in
all the countries of the world.

Have you ever thought about visiting a world like this, or
imagined that tiny people are living their own lives in
hedgerows, the nooks and crannies of old houses or even
under your feet?

 **In this unit you will read and talk about some of
these stories before writing about a small world
of your own.**

Small in a big world

Read this extract from *The Little Man* by Erich Kästner. It is about Maxie, a midget who lives with Professor Hokus von Pokus and works in a circus.

The little man

At night Maxie slept in a matchbox. Instead of the forty matches such a box normally holds, it contained a tiny cotton-wool mattress, a small strip of camel-hair counterpane and a pillow no larger than the nail on my middle finger. And the box was left half-open, because otherwise the poor little chap wouldn't have been able to breathe.

The matchbox stood on the bedside table next to the conjurer's bed. And every night, when Professor Hokus von Pokus had turned over to face the wall and begun to snore softly, Maxie would switch off the bedside lamp on the bedside table, and it would not be long before he was asleep too.

The two doves, Minna and Emma, and Alba, the white rabbit in his wicker basket, all slept in the same hotel room as Maxie and the Professor. The doves would perch on the top of the wardrobe. They would hide their heads in their breast feathers, and when they dreamed they used to coo.

The three animals belonged to the Professor and helped him in his performance in the circus. The doves would suddenly flutter out of the sleeves of his tail-coat, and he would magic the rabbit out of his empty top-hat. Minna, Emma and Alba were very fond of the Professor and they were simply devoted to the little boy. After they had had breakfast at five in the morning, Maxie was even sometimes allowed to sit on Emma's back, and then she would take him for a flip round the room.

A matchbox is two and a quarter inches long, an inch and a half wide and three-quarters of an inch high. It was just the right size for Maxie. For even at the age of ten or twelve he only measured two inches precisely, and just fitted nicely into the box. On the hotel desk-clerk's letter-balance he weighed only two ounces, yet he always had a good appetite and had never been ill. He'd had the measles, to be sure. But the measles don't really count. Nearly every child in creation has *them*.

At the age of seven he naturally wanted to start school. But the difficulties were all too great. For one thing, every time the circus moved on he would have had to change schools. And often even change his language, too! For in Germany the teaching was in German, in England it was in English, in France it was in French, in Italy it was in Italian and in Norway it was in Norwegian. The Little Man might well have managed even that, for he was brighter than most children of his age. But the trouble was that his classmates were all much, much bigger than he, and they flattered themselves that being bigger was something special. So he had to put with a lot, the poor chap.

In Athens, for example, during the lunch break, three little Greek girls popped him into an inkwell. And in Brussels a couple of Belgian louts stuck him on the curtain-rod. Nevertheless, he climbed down again at once. Because even at that age he could already climb better than anyone. But he had not cared for such stupid tricks at all. And so the conjuror suggested to

him one day: 'Do you know what? The best thing would be for me to give you private lessons.'

'Oh, wonderful!' Maxie cried. 'That's a good idea! When do we start?'

'Tomorrow morning at nine,' replied Professor Hokus von Pokus. 'But don't start grinning too soon!'

It took some time before they found out the most convenient way to arrange things. But gradually they solved their problems, and then, day by day, they began to get more and more fun from their lessons. The most important things, beside the reader and the exercise-book, were a pair of folding steps and a strong magnifying-glass.

In the reading lesson, Maxie would scramble up on to the step-ladder's topmost step, because if he sat with his nose in the book the letters were too big for him. Only when he was perched on top of the steps could he read the print in comfort.

For writing, it was just the opposite. Then he had to sit at a tiny desk. The tiny desk stood on the big table. And the Professor would sit at the table and scan Maxie's scritch-scratch through the magnifying-glass. It enlarged the writing seven times, and this was the only way he could make anything at all of the letters and the words. Without the magnifying-glass, he and the bedroom waiter and the maids would have mistaken the scratchings for ink-splashes. And yet, as one could see quite clearly by using the magnifying-glass, the letters were prettily and delicately formed.

It was the same in the arithmetic lesson. For numbers, too, they used the steps and the

magnifying-glass. And so Maxie, whether he learnt anything or not, was always on the move. Now he would be sitting on the steps, now at his desk.

One fine morning, the bedroom waiter, who had come to take away the breakfast things, remarked: 'If I didn't know for sure that the young gentleman was learning to read and write, I would certainly think he was taking lessons in gymnastics.' They all had to laugh at that. Even Minna and Emma, who were perched on the wardrobe, chortled with them. For they were chortle doves.

Maxie did not take long to learn his letters. After a very short time, he could read as fluently as if he'd been doing it all his life. And then he became, almost overnight, a bookworm. The first book that Hokus von Pokus gave him was *Grimm's Fairy Tales*. And quite probably he would have read them all within a week, if it had not been for those dratted folding-steps!

Every time he wanted to turn a page, there was nothing for it but to clamber down the steps, jump down on to the table, turn the page, then scramble to the top of the steps again. That was the only way he could proceed with the story. And after reading those two pages he had to

climb down again to reach the book! So this was the procedure: turn page, up steps, read two sides, down steps, on to the table, turn page quickly, up steps, read next two sides, down ladder, turn page, up – it was enough to wear one out!

One afternoon the Professor came in just as the boy was crawling up the steps for the twenty-third time, tearing his hair with rage and shouting: 'It's really awful! For heaven's sake, why aren't there any smaller books? With weeny letters?'

Erich Kästner (from *The Little Man*)

Look back on your reading. What effect does Maxie's size have on his life and education?

Answering these questions will help you:

- What can you find out about what Maxie looks like?

- Where does Maxie sleep?

- What does he enjoy about his small life?

- What are the problems of being so small?

- What makes reading and writing difficult?

2 Big in a small world

> Read this extract from *Gulliver's Travels* by Jonathan Swift. This extract tells how Gulliver helps the tiny Lilliputians defeat their enemies, the Blefuscudians.

Tying up the fleet

I communicated to his Majesty a project I had formed of seizing the enemy's whole fleet; which lay at anchor in the harbour ready to sail with the first fair wind. I consulted the most experienced seamen upon the depth of the channel, who told me, that in the middle at high water it was seventy *glumgluffs* deep, which is about six foot of European measure; and the rest of it fifty *glumgluffs* at most. I walked to the north-east coast where, lying down behind a hillock, I took out my small pocket glass, and viewed the enemy's fleet at anchor, consisting of about fifty men-of-war, and a great number of transports: I then came back to my house, and gave order for a great quantity of the strongest cable and bars of iron. The cable was about as thick as thread, and the bars of the length and size of a knitting-needle. I trebled the cable to make it stronger, and for the same reason I twisted three of the iron bars together, bending the extremities into a hook. Having fixed fifty hooks to as many cables, I went back to the north-east coast, and putting off my coat, shoes, and stockings, walked into the sea in my leathern jerkin, about half an hour before high water.

I waded with what haste I could, and swam in the middle about thirty yards till I felt ground; I arrived at the fleet in less than half an hour. The enemy was so frighted when they saw me, that they leaped out of their ships, and swam to shore, where there could not be fewer than thirty thousand souls. I then took my tackling, and fastening a hook to the hole at the prow of each, I tied all the cords together at the end. While I was thus employed, the enemy discharged several thousand arrows, many of which stuck in my hands and face; and besides the excessive smart, gave me much disturbance in my work. My greatest apprehension was for mine eyes, which I should have infallibly lost, if I had not suddenly thought of an expedient. I kept among other little necessaries a pair of spectacles in a private pocket, which, as I observed before, had escaped the Emperor's searchers. These I took out and fastened as strongly as I could upon my nose, and thus armed went on boldly with my work in spite of the enemy's arrows, many of which struck against the glasses of my spectacles, but without any other effect, further than a little to discompose them. I had now fastened all the hooks, and taking the knot in my hand, began to pull; but not a ship would stir, for they were all too fast held by their anchors, so that the

boldest part of my enterprise remained. I therefore let go the cord, and leaving the hooks fixed to the ships, I resolutely cut with my knife the cables that fastened the anchors, receiving above two hundred shots in my face and hands; then I took up the knotted end of the cables to which my hooks were tied, and with great ease drew fifty of the enemy's largest men-of-war after me.

The Blefuscudians, who had not the least imagination of what I intended, were at first confounded with astonishment. They had seen me cut the cables, and thought my design was only to let the ships run adrift, or fall foul on each other: but when they perceived the whole fleet moving in order, and saw me pulling at the end, they set up such a scream of grief and despair, that it is almost impossible to describe or conceive. When I had got out of danger, I stopped a while to pick out the arrows that stuck in my hands and face, and rubbed on some of the same ointment that was given me at my first arrival, as I have formerly mentioned. I then took off my spectacles, and waiting about an hour till the tide was a little fallen, I waded through the middle with my cargo, and arrived safe at the royal port of Lilliput.

The Emperor and his whole Court stood on the shore expecting the issue of this great adventure. They saw the ships move forward in a large half-moon, but could not discern me, who was up to my breast in water. When I advanced to the middle of the channel, they were yet more in pain, because I was under water to my neck. The Emperor concluded me to be drowned, and that the enemy's fleet was approaching in a hostile manner: but he was soon eased of his fears, for the channel growing shallower every step I made, I came in a short time within hearing, and holding up the end of the cable by which the fleet was fastened, I cried in a loud voice, *Long live the most puissant Emperor of Lilliput!* This great prince received me at my landing with all possible encomiums, and created me a *Nardac* upon the spot, which is the highest title of honour among them.

Jonathan Swift (from Gulliver's Travels)

Working as a group of four, look back on your reading.

Answer these questions:

- How does Gulliver's size help him defeat the Blefuscudians?

- What impression does the extract give of Gulliver's character?

- What do you think the story is saying about weapons and wars between nations?

- Does it have a message for today's world?

Each of you should choose one question and report your ideas back to the class.

3 Facing dangers in the big world

Being small in a world where everything is big can be dangerous.

> Read these extracts from *The Borrowers Afloat* by Mary Norton, *Truckers* by Terry Pratchett and *The Lord of the Rings* by J R R Tolkien.

Almost poached!

The borrowers are miniature people who live under the floorboards of houses. They 'borrow' the things that big people lose. In this extract, the borrowers have left the safety of their house.

They ate their supper on the up-stream side of the island where the ripples broke at their feet and where the kettle, tied on its side, had risen clear of the water. The level of the stream was sinking fast and the water seemed far less muddy.

'What's that?' said Homily suddenly, gazing down at the ripples, 'something pink ...'

They followed the direction of her eyes. Just below the surface something wriggled, held up against the current.

'It's a worm,' said Arrietty after a moment. Homily stared at it thoughtfully. 'You said right, Pod,' she admitted after a moment. 'I have changed ... '

'In what way?' asked Pod.

'Looking at that worm,' said Homily, 'all scoured and scrubbed, like – clean as a whistle – I was thinking.' She hesitated. 'Well, I was thinking ... I could eat a worm like that ... '

'What, raw?' exclaimed Pod, amazed.

'No, stewed of course,' retorted Homily crossly, 'with a bit of wild garlic.' She stared again at the water. 'What's it caught up on?'

Pod craned forward. 'I can't quite see ... ' Suddenly his face became startled and his gaze, sharply intent, slid away on a rising curve towards the bushes.

'What's the matter, Pod?' asked Homily.

He looked at her aghast – a slow stare. 'Someone's fishing,' he breathed, scarcely above his breath.

'Where?' whispered Homily.

Pod jerked his head towards the stunted willows. 'There – behind those bushes ... '

Then Homily, raising her eyes at last, made out the fishing line. Arrietty saw it too. Only in glimpses was it visible: not at all under water but against the surface here and there. They perceived the hair-thin shadow. As it rose it became invisible again, lost against the dimness of the willows, but they could follow its direction.

'Can't see nobody,' whispered Homily.

'Course you can't!' snapped Pod. 'A trout's got eyes, remember, just like you and me ... '

'Not *just* like – ' protested Homily.

'You don't want to show yourself,' Pod went on, 'not when you're fishing.'

'Especially when you're poaching,' put in Arrietty. Why are we whispering? she wondered. Our voices can't be heard above the voices of the river.

'That's right, lass,' said Pod, 'especially if you're poaching. And that's just what he is, I shouldn't wonder – a poacher.'

'What's a poacher?' whispered Homily.

Pod hushed her, raising his hand: 'Quiet, Homily,' and then he added aside: 'A kind of human borrower.'

'A human borrower ... ' repeated Homily in a bewildered whisper: it seemed a contradiction in terms.

'Quiet, Homily,' pleaded Pod.

'He can't hear us,' said Arrietty, 'not from the bank. Look!' she exclaimed. 'The worm's gone.'

So it had, and the line had gone too.

'Wait a minute,' said Pod; 'you'll see – he sends it down on the current.'

Straining their eyes they made out the curves of floating line and, just below the surface, the pinkness of the worm sailing before them.

The worm fetched up in the same spot, just below their feet, where again it was held against the current.

Something flicked out from under the sticks below them: there was a flurry of shadow, a swift half-turn, and most of the worm had gone.

'A fish?' whispered Arrietty.

Pod nodded.

Homily craned forward: she was becoming quite excited. 'Look, Arrietty – now you can see the hook!'

Arrietty caught just a glimpse of it and then the hook was gone.

'He felt that,' said Pod, referring to the fisherman; 'thinks he got a bite.'

'But he did get a bite,' said Arrietty.

'He got a bite but he didn't get a fish. Here it comes again ... '

It was a new worm this time, darker in colour.

Homily shuddered: 'I wouldn't fancy that one, whichever way you cooked it.'

'Quiet, Homily,' said Pod as the worm was whisked away.

'You know,' exclaimed Homily excitedly, 'what we could do – say we had some kind of fire? We could take the fish off the hook and cook and eat it ourselves ... '

'Say there was a fish *on* the hook,' remarked Pod, gazing soberly towards the bushes. Suddenly he gave a cry and ducked sideways, his hands across his face. 'Look out!' he yelled in a frantic voice.

It was too late: there was the hook in Homily's skirt, worm and all. They ran to her, holding her against the pull of the line while her wild shrieks echoed down the river.

'Unbutton it, Homily! Take the skirt off! Quick ...'

But Homily couldn't or wouldn't. It might have had something to do with the fact that underneath she was wearing a very short red flannel petticoat which once had belonged to Arrietty and did not think it would look seemly, or she might quite simply just have lost her head. She clung to Pod and, dragged out of his grasp, she clung to Arrietty. Then she clung to the twigs and sticks as she was dragged past them towards the ripples.

They got her out of the water as the line for a moment went slack, and Arrietty fumbled with the small jet bead which served Homily's skirt as a button. Then the line went taut again. As Pod grabbed hold of Homily he saw out of the corner of his eye that the fisherman was standing up.

From this position, on the very edge of the bank, he could play his rod more freely: a sudden upward jerk and Homily, caught by her skirt and shrieking loudly, flew upside-down into the air with Pod and Arrietty fiercely clinging each to an arm. Then the jet button burst off, the skirt sailed away with the worm, and the borrowers, in a huddle, fell back on the sticks. The sticks sank slightly beneath the impact and rose again as gently, breaking the force of their fall.

'That was a near one,' gasped Pod, pulling his leg out of a cleft between the branches. Arrietty, who had come down on her seat, remained sitting: she seemed shaken but unhurt. Homily, crossing her arms, tenderly massaged her shoulders: she had a long graze on her cheek and a jagged tear in the red flannel petticoat. 'You all right, Homily?'

Homily nodded, and her bun unrolled slowly. White-faced and shaking she felt mechanically for hairpins: she was staring fixedly at the fisherman.

'It's Mild Eye,' she announced grimly after a moment.

Pod swung round, narrowing his eyes. Arrietty stood up to see better: Mild Eye, the gipsy ... there was no mistaking the ape-like build, the heavy eye-brows, the thatch of greying hair.

'Now we'll be for it,' said Homily.

Pod was silent for a moment. 'He can't get at us here,' he decided at last, 'right out here in mid-stream: the water's good and deep out here, on both sides of us, like.'

'He could stand in the shallows and reach,' said Homily.

'Doubt if he'd make it,' said Pod.

'He knows us and he's seen us,' said Homily in the same expressionless voice. She drew a long, quivering breath: 'And, you mark my words, he's not going to miss us again!'

There was silence except for the voices of the river. The babbling murmur, unperturbed and even, seemed suddenly alien and heartless.

'Why doesn't he move?' asked Arrietty.

'He's thinking,' said Homily.

After a moment, Arrietty ventured timidly: 'Of what he's going to charge for us, and that, when he's got us in a cage?'

'Of what he's going to do next,' said Homily.

They were silent for a moment, watching Mild Eye.

'Look,' said Arrietty.

'What's he up to now?' asked Pod.

'He's taking the skirt off the hook!'

'And the worm too,' said Pod. 'Look out!' he cried as the fisherman's arm flew up. There was a sudden jerk among the sticks, a shuddering series of elastic quivers. 'He's casting for us!' shouted Pod. 'Better we get under cover.'

'No,' said Homily as their island became still again; she watched the caught branch, hooked loose, bobbing away down-river. 'Say he drags this obstruction to bits, we're safer on top than below. Better we take to the kettle – '

But even as she spoke the next throw caught the cork in the rust-hole. The kettle, hooked by its stopper and tied to the sticks, resisted the drag of the rod: they clung together in silent panic as just below them branches began to slide. Then the cork bounced free and leapt away on the end of the dancing line. Their island subsided again and, unclasping each other, they moved apart, listening wide-eyed to the rhythmic gurgle of water filling the kettle.

The next throw caught a key branch, one on which they stood. They could see the hook well and truly in, and the trembling strain on the twine. Pod clambered alongside and, leaning back, tugged downwards against the pull. But strain as he might, the line stayed taut and the hook as deeply embedded.

'Cut it,' cried someone above the creaking and groaning. 'Cut it ... ' the voice cried again tremulously faint, like the rippling voice of the river.

'Then give me the razor-blade,' gasped Pod. Arrietty brought it in a breathless scramble. There was a gentle twang and they all ducked down as the severed line flew free. 'Now why,' exclaimed Pod, 'didn't I think of that in the first place?'

He glanced towards the shore. Mild Eye was reeling in; the line, too light now, trailed softly on the breeze.

'He's not very pleased,' said Homily.

'No,' agreed Pod, sitting down beside her, 'he wouldn't be.'

'Don't think he's got another hook,' said Homily.

They watched Mild Eye examine the end of his line and they met his baleful glare as, angrily raising his head, he stared across the water.

'Round one to us,' said Pod.

Mary Norton (from *The Borrowers Afloat*)

The Thing

The nomes are a race of tiny people who are dying out as a result of pollution and the changes to the environment. In this extract, they are trying to escape from the city, taking the 'Thing' with them for good luck.

The sky rained dismal. It rained humdrum. It rained the kind of rain that is so much wetter than normal rain, the kind of rain that comes down in big drops and splats, the kind of rain that is merely an upright sea with slots in it.

It rained a tattoo on the old hamburger boxes and chip papers in the wire basket that was giving Masklin a temporary hiding place.

Look at him. Wet. Cold. Extremely worried. And four inches high.

The waste-bin was usually a good hunting ground, even in winter. There were often a few cold chips in their wrapping, sometimes even a chicken bone. Once or twice there had been a rat, too. It had been a really good day when there had last been a rat – it had kept them going for a week. The trouble was that you could get pretty fed up with rat by the third day. By the third mouthful, come to that.

Masklin scanned the lorry park.

And here it came, right on time, crashing through the puddles and pulling up with a hiss of brakes.

He'd watched this lorry arrive every Tuesday and Thursday morning for the last four weeks. He timed the driver's stop carefully.

They had exactly three minutes. To someone the size of a nome, that's more than half an hour.

He scrambled down through the greasy paper, dropped out of the bottom of the bin, and ran for the bushes at the edge of the park where Grimma and the old folk were waiting.

'It's here!' he said. 'Come on!'

They got to their feet, groaning and grumbling. He'd taken them through this dozens of times. He knew it wasn't any good shouting. They just got upset and confused, and then they'd grumble some more. They grumbled about cold chips, even when Grimma warmed them up. They moaned about rat. He'd seriously thought about leaving alone, but he couldn't bring himself to do it. They needed him. They needed someone to grumble at.

But they were too *slow*. He felt like bursting into tears.

He turned to Grimma instead.

'Come *on*,' he said. 'Give them a prod, or something. They'll never get moving!'

She patted his hand.

'They're frightened,' she said. 'You go on. I'll bring them out.'

There wasn't time to argue. Masklin ran back across the soaking mud of the park, unslinging the rope and grapnel. It had taken him a week to make the hook out of a bit of wire teased off a fence, and he'd spent days practising; he was already swinging it around his head as he reached the lorry's wheel.

The hook caught the tarpaulin high above him at the second try. He tested it once or twice and then, his feet scrabbling for a grip on the tyre, pulled himself up.

He'd done it before. Oh, he'd done it three or four times. He scrambled under the heavy tarpaulin and into the darkness beyond, pulling out more line and tying it as tightly as possible around one of the ropes that were as thick as his arm.

Then he slid back to the edge and, thank goodness, Grimma *was* herding the old people across the gravel. He could hear them complaining about the puddles.

Masklin jumped up and down with impatience.

It seemed to take hours. He explained it to them millions of times, but people hadn't been pulled up on to the backs of lorries when they were children and they didn't see why they should start now. Old Granny Morkie insisted that all the men look the other way so that they wouldn't see up her skirts, for example, and old Torrit whimpered so much that Masklin had to lower him again so that Grimma could blindfold him. It wasn't so bad after he'd hauled the first few up, because they were able to help on the rope, but time still stretched out.

He pulled Grimma up last. She was light. They were *all* light, if it came to that. You didn't get rat every day.

It was amazing. They were all on board. He'd worked with an ear cocked for the sound of foot steps on gravel and the slamming of the driver's door, and it hadn't happened.

'Right,' he said, shaking with the effort. 'That's it, then. Now if we just go – '

'I dropped the Thing,' said old Torrit. 'The Thing. I dropped it, d'you see? I dropped it down by the wheel when she was blindfoldin' me. You go and get it, boy.'

Masklin looked at him in horror. Then he poked his head out from under the tarpaulin and, yes, there it was, far below. A tiny black cube on the ground.

The Thing.

It was lying in a puddle, although that wouldn't affect it. Nothing touched the Thing. It wouldn't even burn.

And then he heard the sound of slow footsteps on the gravel.

'There's no time,' he whispered. 'There really is no time.'

'We can't go without it,' said Grimma.

'Of course we can. It's just a, a thing. We won't need the wretched object where we're going.'

He felt guilty as soon as he'd said it, amazed at his own lips for uttering such words. Grimma looked horrified. Granny Morkie drew herself up to her full, quivering height.

'May you be forgiven!' she barked. 'What a terrible thing to say! You tell him, Torrit.' She nudged Torrit in the ribs.

'If we ain't taking the Thing, I ain't going,' said Torrit sulkily. 'It's not – '

'That's your leader talkin' to you,' interrupted Granny Morkie. 'So you do what you're told. Leave it behind, indeed! It wouldn't be decent. It wouldn't be right. So you go and get it this minute.'

Masklin stared wordlessly down at the soaking mud and then, with a desperate motion, threw the line over the edge and slid down it.

It was raining harder now, with a touch of sleet. The wind whipped at him as he dropped past the great arc of the wheel and landed heavily in the puddle. He reached out and scooped up the Thing And the lorry started to move.

First there was a roar, so loud that it went beyond

67

sound and became a solid wall of noise. Then there was a blast of stinking air and a vibration that shook the ground.

He pulled sharply on the line and yelled at them to pull him up, and realised that even he couldn't hear his own voice. But Grimma or someone must have got the idea because, just as the big wheel began to turn, the rope tightened and he felt his feet lifted off the mud.

He bounced and spun back and forth as, with painful slowness, they pulled him past the wheel. It turned only a few inches away from him, a black, chilly blur, and all the time the hammering sound battered at his head.

I'm not scared, he told himself. This is much worse than anything I've ever faced, and it's not frightening. It's too terrible to be frightening.

He felt as though he was in a tiny, warm cocoon, away from all the noise and the wind. I'm going to die, he thought, just because of this Thing which has never helped us at all, something that's just a lump of stuff, and now I'm going to die and go to the Heavens. I wonder if old Torrit is right about what happens when you die? It seems a bit severe to have to die to find out. I've looked at the sky every night for years and I've never seen any nomes up there ...

But it didn't really matter, it was all outside him, it wasn't real –

Hands reached down and caught him under the arms and dragged him into the booming space under the tarpaulin and, with some difficulty, prised the Thing out of his grip.

Behind the speeding lorry fresh curtains of grey rain dragged across the empty fields.

Terry Pratchett (from *Truckers*)

The Black Riders

Hobbits are medium-sized creatures. They lived a quiet life in the rural Shire until one of them, Frodo, inherits a powerful magic ring. Now, the forces of evil are seeking the Ring and wanting to use its power for themselves.

They stood for a while silent on the hill-top, near its southward edge. In that lonely place Frodo for the first time fully realised his homelessness and danger. He wished bitterly that his fortune had left him in the quiet and beloved Shire. He stared down at the hateful Road, leading back westward – to his home. Suddenly he was aware that two black specks were moving slowly along it, going westward; and looking again he saw that three others were creeping eastward to meet them. He gave a cry and clutched Strider's arm.

'Look,' he said, pointing downwards.

At once Strider flung himself on the ground behind the ruined circle, pulling Frodo down beside him. Merry threw himself alongside.

'What is it?' he whispered.

'I do not know, but I fear the worst,' answered Strider.

Slowly they crawled up to the edge of the ring again, and peered through a cleft between two jagged stones. The light was no longer bright, for the clear morning had faded, and clouds creeping out of the East had now overtaken the sun, as it began to go down. They could all see the black specks, but neither Frodo nor Merry could make out their shapes for certain; yet something told them that there, far below, were Black Riders assembling on the Road beyond the foot of the hill.

'Yes,' said Strider, whose keener sight left him in no doubt. 'The enemy is here!'

Hastily they crept away and slipped down the north side of the hill to find their companions.

Down in the longest and most sheltered corner of the dell they lit a fire, and prepared a meal. The shades of evening began to fall, and it grew cold. They were suddenly aware of great hunger, for they had not eaten since breakfast; but they dared not make more than a frugal supper. The lands ahead were empty of all save birds and beasts, unfriendly places deserted by all the races of the world. Rangers passed at times beyond the hills, but they were few and did not stay. Other wanderers were rare, and of evil sort: trolls might stray down at times out of the northern valleys of the Misty Mountains. Only on the Road would travellers be found, most often dwarves, hurrying along on business of their own, and with no help and few words to spare for strangers.

'I don't see how our food can be made to last,' said Frodo. 'We have been careful enough in the last few days, and this supper is no feast; but we have used more than we ought, if we have two weeks still to go, and perhaps more.'

'There is food in the wild,' said Strider; 'berry, root, and herb; and I have some skill as a hunter at need. You need not be afraid of starving before winter comes. But gathering and catching food is long and weary work, and we need haste. So tighten your belts, and think with hope of the tables of Elrond's house!'

The cold increased as darkness came on. Peering out from the edge of the dell they could see nothing but a grey land now vanishing quickly into shadow. The sky had cleared again and was slowly filled with twinkling stars. Frodo and his companions huddled round the fire, wrapped in every garment and blanket they possessed; but Strider was content with a single cloak, and sat a

little apart, drawing thoughtfully at his pipe.

Each of the hobbits saw in his mind a vision of the cloaked and booted Riders. If the horsemen had already found the dell, the sooner Strider led them somewhere else the better. Sam viewed the hollow with great dislike, now that he had heard news of their enemies on the Road, only a few miles away.

'Can the Riders *see*?' asked Merry. 'I mean, they seem usually to have used their noses rather than their eyes, smelling for us, if smelling is the right word, at least in the daylight. But you made us lie down flat when you saw them down below; and now you talk of being seen, if we move.'

'I was too careless on the hill-top,' answered Strider. 'I was very anxious to find some sign of Gandalf; but it was a mistake for three of us to go up and stand there so long. For the black horses can see, and the Riders can use men and other creatures as spies. They themselves do not see the world of light as we do, but our shapes cast shadows in their minds, which only the noon sun destroys; and in the dark they perceive many signs and forms that are hidden from us: then they are most to be feared. And at all times they smell the blood of living things, desiring and hating it. Senses, too, there are other than sight or smell. We can feel their presence – it troubled our hearts, as soon as we came here, and before we saw them; they feel ours more keenly. Also,' he added, and his voice sank to a whisper, 'the Ring draws them.'

'Is there no escape then?' said Frodo, looking round wildly. 'If I move I shall be seen and hunted! If I stay, I shall draw them to me!'

Strider laid his hand on his shoulder. 'There is still hope.'

As Strider was speaking they watched his strange eager face, dimly lit in the red glow of the wood-fire. His eyes shone, and his voice was rich and deep. Above him was a black starry sky. Suddenly a pale light appeared over the crown of Weathertop behind him. The waxing moon was climbing slowly above the hill that overshadowed them, and the stars above the hill-top faded.

The hobbits moved and stretched. 'Look!' said Merry. 'The moon is rising: it must be getting late.'

The others looked up. Even as they did so, they saw on the top of the hill something small and dark against the glimmer of the moon-rise. It was perhaps only a large stone or jutting rock shown up by the pale light.

Sam and Merry got up and walked away from the fire. Frodo and Pippin remained seated in silence. Strider was watching the moon-light on the hill intently. All seemed quiet and still, but Frodo felt a cold dread creeping over his heart. He huddled closer to the fire. At that moment Sam came running back from the edge of the dell.

'I don't know what it is,' he said, 'but I suddenly felt afraid. I durstn't go outside this dell for any money; I felt that something was creeping up the slope.'

'Did you *see* anything?' asked Frodo, springing to his feet.

'No, sir. I saw nothing, but I didn't stop to look.'

'I saw something,' said Merry; 'or I thought I did – away westwards where the moonlight was falling on the flats behind the shadow of the hill-tops, I *thought* there were two or three black shapes. They seemed to be coming this way.'

'Keep close to the fire, with your faces outward!' cried Strider. 'Get some of the longer sticks ready in your hands!'

For a breathless time they sat there, silent and alert, with their backs turned to the wood-fire, each gazing into the shadows that encircled them. Nothing happened. There was no sound or movement in the night. Frodo stirred, feeling that he must break the silence: he longed to shout out aloud.

'Hush!' whispered Strider. 'What's that?' gasped Pippin at the same moment.

Over the top of the little dell, on the side away from the hill, they felt, rather than saw, a shadow rise, one shadow or more than one. They strained their eyes, and the shadows seemed to grow. Soon there could be no doubt: three or four tall black figures were standing there on the slope, looking down on them. So black were

was bitter cold, but his terror was swallowed up in a sudden temptation to put on the Ring. The desire to do this laid hold of him, and he could not think of anything else. He did not forget the Barrow, nor the message of Gandalf; but something seemed to be compelling him to disregard all warnings, and he longed to yield. Not with the hope of escape, or of doing anything, either good or bad: he simply felt that he must take the Ring and put it on his finger. He could not speak. He felt Sam looking at him, as if he knew that his master was in some great trouble, but he could not turn towards him. He shut his eyes and struggled for a while; but resistance became unbearable, and at last he slowly drew out the chain, and slipped the Ring on the forefinger of his left hand.

Immediately, though everything else remained as before, dim and dark, the shapes became terribly clear. He was able to see beneath their black wrappings. There were five tall figures: two standing on the lip of the dell, three advancing. In their white faces burned keen and merciless eyes; under their mantles were long grey robes; upon their grey hairs were helms of silver; in their haggard hands were swords of steel. Their eyes fell on him and pierced him, as they rushed towards him. Desperate, he drew his own sword, and it seemed to him that it flickered red, as if it was a firebrand. Two of the figures halted. The third was taller than the others: his hair was long and gleaming and on his helm was a crown. In one hand he held a long sword, and in the other a knife; both the knife and the hand that held it glowed with a pale light. He sprang forward and bore down on Frodo.

J R R Tolkien (from *The Fellowship of the Ring*)

they that they seemed like black holes in the deep shade behind them. Frodo thought that he heard a faint hiss as of venomous breath and felt a thin piercing chill. Then the shapes slowly advanced.

Terror overcame Pippin and Merry, and they threw themselves flat on the ground. Sam shrunk to Frodo's side. Frodo was hardly less terrified than his companions; he was quaking as if he

Compare the extracts by answering these questions:

- What are you *told* about the small people in each of the extracts?

- What are they called? What do they look like?

- What kind of people are they? What can you find out about their characters?

- What are the dangers they face? What are the big people around them like?

... on how to write about what you read

In English lessons, you are often asked to write about a story you have read. You are asked to show that you have understood it or say how it has affected you.

These are some of the questions you might be asked, and the kind of answers you should try to give in your writing:

Q: What did you read?
A: Give the title and say who the author was.

Q: What happened in the piece of writing?
A: Give an account of the plot (the events) and the names of the characters.

Q: What impression does the story give of people and places?
A: Say something about the characters and the setting.

Q: What did you find the most exciting or interesting part?
A: Say what it was and why you liked it.

Q: What were the best descriptions of what happened?
A: Say what these were. Give some examples of the descriptive language or comparisons.

Q: What impression did the story make on you?
A: Say what you think and back up your views with examples or a quotation.

Skills box

Writing as if you were there

You may be asked to continue a story or write as if you lived at some time in the past, in another country or another place. If you are going to bring that place and time to life, you have to use your imagination.

Follow these steps for success:

Read the story or stimulus material very carefully
Don't rely on your memory.
Make notes about what happens, who the characters are and what you can find out about the background.
Note the small details as well as the obvious ones.

Use your imagination to add to what you have read
Look for clues in your reading as to what happens next.
Which of these characters are brave?
Who might run away from trouble?
Think about the sorts of things that would be likely to happen in these times and places.

Recreate the mood
If you want to continue a story or to recreate the atmosphere of a time or place, you have to imagine yourself there.

In your mind look around you. What is the landscape like? What do the people look like? What are they wearing?
Think about what you can smell and taste in the air and the feel of objects and materials in your characters' hands.

Write your narrative
Never try to make too much happen in your writing.
Focus on your characters and how they react to a few events.
If you put them in danger, plan an escape so that your story can continue.

Redraft, revise and proof-read
As you do this, add details which make your story more realistic and authentic.
Make sure that you spell the names of the characters correctly whenever you write them.
Add conversations and arguments to your writing.

4 Continue the story

All of the extracts you have just read are about journeys that small people make in big worlds.

Choose one of them and write about another episode that involves these characters. Write about what happens to:

- The Borrowers (Pod, Arrietty and Homily) when they meet up again with Mild Eye or face a wild animal

- The Nomes (Masklin, Grimma, Granny Morkie and Old Torrit) when the lorry reaches the city

- The Hobbits (Frodo, Merry, Pippin and Sam) after they are separated from their man-friend, Strider, and have another encounter with the Black Riders on a lonely moor.

Before you start writing, look at the Skills box on the previous page.

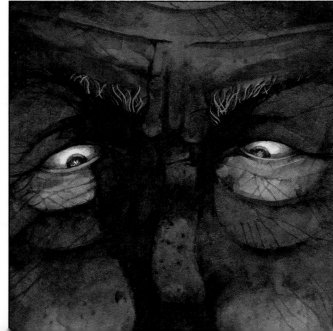

5 Read your stories

Read some of the stories back to the class.

Talk about which of your stories best capture the characters and atmosphere of the original story.

Discuss how they do this.

on target

After working through this unit, could you:

- say why stories about small worlds are so popular?

- comment on a book or story you were asked to read?

- continue a story with greater confidence?

School dinners

How have school meals changed over the years? Are young people at all worried about the effect their diet can have on their health, now and in the future? How can healthy eating be encouraged?

 In this unit you will carry out a survey to see how eating habits have changed over the years. You will write up your findings as a report and as a newspaper article. You will design a poster or leaflet.

Find out about school meals in the past

Until very recently, almost every child was able to have a free meal at school. The free meal was one way of making sure that every child had a healthy diet. Today, only four children out of ten eat school lunches.

Try to find out more about school meals in the past. Ask relatives and family friends who were at school in, or before, 1970 what they remember about their school meals. Make notes of what you find out.

You could ask about:

- their favourite meals
- the meals they hated the most
- coloured blancmange
- the skin on milk puddings
- school milk on hot days
- cabbage
- 'tables' and 'servers'
- second helpings
- 'centralised' kitchens
- left-overs.

Write a brief report of your findings.

2 Find out about school meals today

Read this magazine article about what young people are eating in a typical secondary school today.

Too much fat, too little fibre

It's 1 pm and 12-year-old James is about to tuck into lunch – a honey sandwich, a packet of crisps and some biscuits he has just bought from the school tuck shop. This is his third sugar binge of the day. For breakfast he had a bowl of Sugar Puffs and mid-morning he tucked into a couple of Bart Simpson biscuits. Later on he'll round off his evening meal with ice cream and a can of Coke.

James is not unusual. When we asked a class of 11 and 12 year olds to write down everything they'd had to eat and drink the day before, we were horrified that over a quarter had eaten no fresh fruit or vegetables. And only a handful came near the four portions that the World Health Organisation (WHO) recommends everyone should eat daily. One boy managed to plough through a piece of pizza, a burger and a hot dog half-way through the morning. Then he stashed away three burgers, chips and three chocolate milkshakes at lunchtime, and it wasn't as though he was short of food at home. For breakfast he had two croissants, and his evening meal was a roast. It was not unusual for these children to get through three packets of crisps a day. In the worst cases, these were teamed with chips from the canteen at midday.

It's little wonder that there's mounting concern about the quality of our children's diets. Studies repeatedly show that children eat too much fat and sugar and too little fibre, fruit and vegetables. Many are also short of essential vitamins and minerals. And a major cause of such bad habits is what these children eat at school.

Most junior schools still provide a set-price lunch of a main course with vegetables and a dessert, but secondary schools tend to operate a cash cafeteria system, which offers a few main meals such as cottage pie, lasagne or salads, plus stodgy favourites such as burgers and chips teamed with chocolate and crisps from the tuck shop.

When *Which?* magazine conducted a survey of 120 schoolchildren and 450 parents in September they found that junior schools' meals were still reasonably nutritious (although low in fibre). But in secondary school canteens, which often compete with local shops, vans and takeaways, the story was different. These teenagers tended to eat foods that were high in fat and sugar and low in fibre, iron and folate (particularly important for teenage girls). Half the children ate packed lunches but, again, these were unusually high in fat and sugar and low in fibre. Only one in four contained fruit. Most secondary schoolchildren supplemented this with unhealthy snacks and drinks from the canteen, tuck shop or vending machine.

Sue Platt

3 Check your reading

What does the magazine article say about healthy and unhealthy foods?

Make a copy of the chart below and complete it.

The healthy things that pupils *should* eat	The unhealthy things that pupils eat
fresh fruit and vegetables	honey sandwich
	crisps
fibre	

Do you agree with what the article says?

Do all schoolchildren have an unhealthy diet? Or do you think the article is being unfair?

Discuss your ideas with your group.

4 A survey – are your friends healthy eaters?

What about you? Are you a healthy eater? What about your friends at school?

The best way to find out is to organise a survey. Follow these steps for success.

1 Decide what you want to find out
In this case, you want to know what the pupils in your school eat during a typical day.

2 Decide what information (data) you will need to show this
You could look at the food people ate yesterday. If today is a Monday, you could ask what they ate over the past weekend.

3 Make sure your data is reliable
You must ask everyone in your survey exactly the same questions. This will make sure that your survey is as accurate as possible.

Imagine you asked some people what *meals* they had on one day, and others what they *ate* on that day. The second group might mention the snacks they had between meals, but the first group would not do so. You would have collected data that was not accurate.

4 Design a questionnaire
A questionnaire is the name for the list of questions you are going to ask people. In this case, the easiest way to organise your questions might be to work through the day. If you used

this approach, these are the kinds of question you might ask people:

> What did you have for breadfast?
> What did you eat mid-morning? at lunch-time? Mid-afternoon? Tea-time In the evening?
> Did you have sweets, biscuits, ice-cream or snacks at any other time?

If you asked the questions like this, you would have trouble writing down the answers. You would have to write a different account for each person.

You want to make it as easy as possible for you to note down the answers and to go over them again later. The best way of doing this is to leave enough space after each question (or by the side of each question) for you to jot down the answer.

What did you have for breakfast? _____

_____

What did you eat mid-morning? _____
At lunch-time? _____

Mid-afternoon? _____
Tea-time? _____
In the evening? _____

Did you have sweets, biscuits, ice-cream or snacks at any other time? Yes/No [and time] _____

Another way to do this is to list the answers that people might give and then ask them to tick or choose the right answer for them. This kind of questionnaire could look like this:

3. Please can you tell me which of these you had for breakfast?

Tea/Coffee ☐
Cereals or porridge ☐
Toast and marmalade, spread or jam ☐
Fruit ☐
Fried food ☐
Snack
Something else (please give details) ————

To save time and paper, you could write the possible responses on a card with numbers or letters and show them to the person. Then, all you have to do is write down the letters or numbers.

What did you have for breakfast?
1. Tea
2. Coffee
3. Cereals or porridge
4. Toast and marmalade, spread or jam
5. Fruit
6. Fried food
7. Snack
8. Something else

You should now be able to design your questionnaire.

5 You need to make sure that you ask enough people

Imagine you only asked two people what they ate. You might find out that one ate yoghurt for breakfast and the other did not. You could not use *this* information to say that 50% of the school ate yoghurt for breakfast.

However, if you asked 200 people, and 100 of them said they ate yoghurt, you could use *that* information to say the same thing.

As a general rule, you need to have at least twenty sets of replies.

6 Make sure you ask a wide range of people

If you only ask Year 7 pupils about what they eat at school you will only get part of the picture. By asking all sorts of different people at school, you might find out that different groups of people have different eating habits.

Your teacher could help you, or other members of your class, to look at different samples of people. You could try asking:

- Sixth-formers
- Teachers
- Dining room assistants
- Year 11 pupils.

You should now be ready to carry out your survey.

... on what to do in surveys, and what not to do

- Work in pairs, especially when you are interviewing people you don't know well.

- Always be polite. Ask people if they have time to help you with your questionnaire.

- Don't rush people.

- Don't cheat by inventing answers.

- Use a clipboard, if possible, and keep your cards and forms neat.

- If you are not sure what someone says, ask them politely to explain.

5 Prepare your report

First, look closely at the data you have gathered. For instance, your survey might show that eleven people ate breakfast and that nine did not. It is easier to compare results like this if you turn them into percentages. So you could say:

> 45% of people start school on an empty stomach! A new survey, carried out by Samar Damluji, found that only 55% of people at Bridlington High School eat breakfast!

From your data you might be able to show, among other things, the percentages of your sample who:

- eat a cooked breakfast
- eat no breakfast
- eat more than three snacks a day
- don't eat fruit or fresh vegetables regularly
- eat between meals.

When you have looked carefully at your data, you should be able to tell whether the people you interviewed were healthy eaters or not.

Write a report for a school newspaper. Start off with your main findings. Here are two examples:

Year 7 Diet of Doom

The future looks glum for the National Health Service if the results of our survey on diet are anything to go by. We have some top-class unhealthy eaters in our school.

Only 10% eat vegetables at least ...

Year 7s eat their greens!

A new survey conducted in this school shows that – contrary to popular belief – most of our Year 7s eat a sensible diet.

90% say that they eat vegetables at least ...

You also will need to say:

- when and where the survey was carried out

- how many and what sort of people took part

- how the interviews were carried out

- what the results were

- what you think they show.

Think about using bar charts, pie charts or graphs when you are writing up your report. It is often easier for readers to understand your figures if they are presented in this way.

Read the magazine report on the next page to help you plan your writing.

Use a pie-chart if you want to show *percentages(%)*

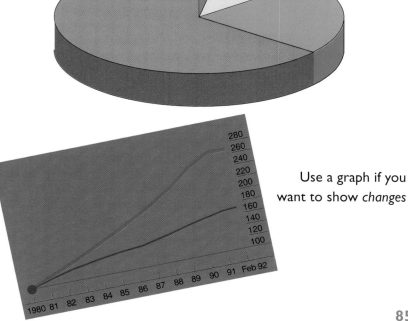

Use a graph if you want to show *changes*

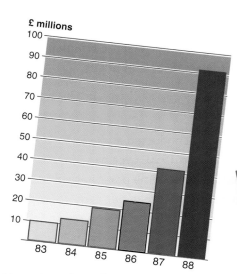

Use a bar chart if you want to show *amounts*

Class of junkies

We asked 25 children in the first year of an East Sussex secondary school to write down exactly what they ate and drank during one day. Here are some of our findings:

- Three girls and two boys ate no breakfast and two girls ate no lunch.

- Fifteen out of the 25 had a sweet snack mid-morning.

- Almost a third ate chips for lunch. Only five ate salad for or with their midday meal (in three cases this was a sandwich). Only three had any fruit for lunch, although four drank a fruit juice.

- A fifth had sweets (excluding chocolate, biscuits, etc.) at some point during the day, and half of them ate a packet of crisps.

The children were taught about nutrition once a fortnight in home economics and knew exactly what they *ought* to eat. They even nicknamed the main serving hatch in the canteen the 'junk bar'. So why didn't they eat well? Most said they 'didn't feel like it'. Many said their evening meal gave them something healthier and more balanced. Some lied to their parents about what they ate at school, and most didn't admit to their sugary snacks.

It didn't help that they were not encouraged to eat well. The children claimed that the salad bar ran out halfway through the lunch break and specials were always snapped up quickly. This left little else besides burger and chips. There wasn't always a vegetarian dish either, and the selection of fresh fruit was poor. As for the drinks, the healthy ones were the most expensive.

Sue Platt

6 Persuade people to eat healthier foods

Here is some more writing about teenagers' eating habits.

The road to illness

If little Johnny has a rotten diet in junior school, he's more likely to be an unhealthy adult. We know that nutritious food is essential for children's development and it can also keep several killer diseases at bay. Yet even though experts tell us constantly that healthy eating habits start young, nutritional standards among schoolchildren have still not improved over the last ten years. In fact, according to some, they've fallen.

Up to 90 per cent of girls are thought to have too little iron and 83 per cent are low in calcium. More than half of children have tooth decay before their second teeth appear. Ten per cent of boys and thirteen per cent of girls are obese at 11 and children as young as three have fatty streaks in their aortas (the main arteries to the heart) from eating too much fat – a sign that they could contract heart disease as adults.

Girls' talk

When MORI conducted a survey of 16- to 19-year-old girls in 1990, over half of them said they'd been on a diet at some point in their lives (compared with sixteen per cent of boys). And almost a quarter of them were trying to lose weight at the time. One expert believes that up to 80 per cent of girls diet or 'binge eat' during their teens and, as we know, some go on to develop

eating disorders – either starving themselves or making themselves sick after eating too much.

Sue Platt

Use this information and your survey findings to start a campaign for better eating in schools.

Design and write one of the following:

- a letter to be sent to parents
- a poster for display in the entrance hall
- a leaflet to be given out to pupils.

Your **purpose** is to persuade your chosen **audience** to eat more healthily.

You will need to think hard about what **form** of writing to choose.

... on writing and designing letters, posters and leaflets

 Letters
- arrive in their reader's hand
- can rely on people taking time to read them
- can make quite complex points
- use mostly text
- are written from one person to another

 Posters
- have to attract a reader's attention
- must be understood at a glance
- convey simple messages
- can use strong pictures
- are impersonal (they are produced with no one person in mind)

 Leaflets
- have to hold a reader's interest
- must be striking and colourful
- make a series of points
- can use a mixture of text and pictures
- can be a mixture of the personal and impersonal

Skills box

Designing and writing posters and leaflets

Posters

The words you use should grab the reader's attention

Use a simple, but striking, image

A slogan that appears on all your pieces of publicity helps to get the message across

A logo will tell people that the poster is part of a wider campaign

Even bears can eat too much honey

Cut down on sugar

Healthy Eating

The facts

Leaflets

An A4 sheet folded into three panels makes a good leaflet

A good mixture of words, pictures and diagrams will make your leaflet attractive

Don't forget your logo!

An attractive cover will encourage people to look into the leaflet

Charts and diagrams give a great deal of information at a glance

healthy eating

As a class, display the results of your work.

Study the materials and decide which letters, posters and leaflets are the most effective. Note down the reasons for your decisions.

Then, compare your ideas with the group's. Do you all agree? Try to reach agreement as a class about which of the materials are the best.

As you do this, you will find that you are talking, in more and more detail, about what makes good writing effective.

on target

After working through this unit, could you:

- prepare a questionnaire (for example, on pocket money and how it is used)?

- give advice to a friend whose eating habits were very unhealthy?

- compare a poster and a leaflet which had both been designed to promote the same cause?

Dear diary

Almost all of us have started a diary at some time in our lives to record events in our lives and our private thoughts and feelings.

In this unit you will study one particular diary written by a young girl caught up in the war in Bosnia. You will write a diary of your own.

Zlata's diary

In September 1991, Zlata Filipović went back to school after the summer holiday and started to keep a diary. She lived in Sarajevo in a part of what had been Yugoslavia. In her diary she talked about her friends and family, her school and her hopes for the future.

Within six months, all this had changed. A vicious civil war broke out in her country, and Sarajevo became a battlefield. Zlata's diary provides her picture of those times.

> Read the extracts below. 'Mimmy' is the name Zlata gave her diary. She wrote as if she were addressing the diary, personally, by this name.

A Bosnian diary

Monday, 2 September 1991
Behind me – a long, hot summer and the happy days of summer holidays; ahead of me – a new school year. I'm starting fifth grade. I'm looking forward to seeing my friends at school, to being together again. Some of them I haven't seen since the day the school bell rang, marking the end of term. I'm glad we'll be together again, and share all the worries and joys of going to school.

Mirna, Bojana, Marijana, Ivana, Maša, Azra, Minela, Nadžsa – we're all together again.

Sunday, 6 October 1991
I'm watching the American Top 20 on MTV. I don't remember a thing, who's in what place.

I feel great because I've just eaten a 'Four Seasons' PIZZA with ham, cheese, ketchup and mushrooms. It was yummy. Daddy bought it for me at Galija's (the pizzeria around the corner). Maybe that's why I didn't remember who took what place – I was too busy enjoying my pizza.

I've finished studying and tomorrow I can go to school BRAVELY, without being afraid of getting a bad grade. I deserve a good grade because I studied all weekend and I didn't even go out to play with my friends in the park. The weather is nice and we usually play 'monkey in the middle', talk and go for walks. Basically, we have fun.

Saturday, 19 October 1991
Yesterday was a really awful day. We were ready to go to Jahorina (the most beautiful mountain in the world) for the weekend. But when I got home from school, I found my mother in tears and my father in uniform. I had a lump in my throat when Daddy said he had been called up by the police reserve. I hugged him, crying, and started begging him not to go, to stay at home. He said he had to go. Daddy went, and Mummy and I were left alone. Mummy cried and phoned friends and relatives. Everyone came immediately (Slobo, Doda, Keka, Mummy's brother Braco, Aunt Melica, there were so many I can't remember them all). They all came to console us and to offer their help. Keka took me to spend the night with Martina and Matea. When I woke up in the morning, Keka told me everything was all right and that Daddy would be home in two days.

I'm home now, Melica is staying with us and it looks as though everything will be all right. Daddy should be home the day after tomorrow. Thank God!

Saturday, 2 May 1992
Dear Mimmy,
Today was truly, absolutely the worst day ever in Sarajevo. The shooting started around noon. Mummy and I moved into the hall. Daddy was in his office, under our flat, at the time. We told him on the interphone to run quickly to the downstairs lobby where we'd meet him. We brought Cicko [Zlata's canary] with us. The gunfire was getting worse, and we couldn't get over the wall to the Bobars, so we ran down to our own cellar.

The cellar is ugly, dark, smelly. Mummy, who's terrified of mice, had two fears to cope with. The three of us were in the same corner as the other day. We listened to the pounding shells, the shooting, the thundering noise overhead. We even heard planes. At one moment I realised that this awful cellar was the only place that could save our lives. Suddenly, it started to look almost warm and nice. It was the only way we could defend ourselves against all this terrible shooting. We heard glass shattering in our street. Horrible. I put my fingers in my ears to block out the terrible sounds. I was worried about Cicko. We had left him behind in the lobby. Would he catch cold there? Would something hit him? I was terribly hungry and thirsty. We had left our half-cooked lunch in the kitchen.

When the shooting died down a bit, Daddy ran over to our flat and brought us back some sandwiches. He said he could smell something burning and that the phones weren't working. He brought our TV set down to the cellar. That's when we learned that the main post office (near us) was on fire and that they had kidnapped our President. At around 10.00 we went back up to our flat. Almost every window in our street was broken. Ours were all right, thank God. I saw the post office in flames. A terrible sight. The fire-fighters battled with the raging fire. Daddy took a few photos of the post office being devoured by the flames. He said they wouldn't come out because I had been fiddling with something on the camera. I was sorry. The whole flat smelled of the burning fire. God, and I used to pass by there every day. It had just been done up. It was huge and beautiful, and now it was being swallowed up by the flames. It was disappearing. That's what this neighbourhood of mine looks like, dear Mimmy. I wonder what it's like in other parts of town? I heard on the radio that it was awful around the Eternal Flame. The place is knee-deep in glass. We're worried about Grandma and Grandad. They live there. Tomorrow, if we can go out, we'll see how they are. A terrible day. This has been the worst, most awful day in my eleven-year-old life. I hope it will be the only one.

Mummy and Daddy are very edgy. I have to go to bed.

Ciao! Zlata

Wednesday, 27 May 1992
Dear Mimmy,
SLAUGHTER! MASSACRE! HORROR! CRIME!
BLOOD! SCREAMS! TEARS! DESPAIR!

That's what Vaso Miskin Street looks like today.
Two shells exploded in the street and one in the
market. Mummy was nearby at the time. She ran
to Grandma's and Grandad's. Daddy and I were
beside ourselves because she hadn't come home.
I saw some of it on TV but I still can't believe what
I actually saw. It's unbelievable. I've got a lump in
my throat and a knot in my tummy. HORRIBLE.
They're taking the wounded to the hospital. It's a
madhouse. We kept going to the window hoping
to see Mummy, but she wasn't back. They
released a list of the dead and wounded. Daddy
and I were tearing our hair out. We didn't know
what had happened to her. Was she alive? At
16.00, Daddy decided to go and check the
hospital. He got dressed, and I got ready to go to
the Bobars', so as not to stay at home alone.
I looked out the window one more time and …
I SAW MUMMY RUNNING ACROSS THE
BRIDGE. As she came into the house she started
shaking and crying. Through her tears she told us
how she had seen dismembered bodies. All the
neighbours came because they had been afraid for
her. Thank God, Mummy is with us. Thank God.

A HORRIBLE DAY. UNFORGETTABLE.
HORRIBLE! HORRIBLE!

Your Zlata

Sunday 17 October 1993
Dear Mimmy,
Yesterday our 'friends in the hills' reminded us of
their presence and that they are now in control
and can kill, wound, destroy … yesterday was a
truly horrible day.

Five hundred and ninety shells. From 4.30 in the
morning on, throughout the day. Six dead and
fifty-six wounded. That is yesterday's toll. Souk-
bunar fared the worst. I don't know how Melica
is. They say that half the houses up there are
gone.

We went down into the cellar. Into the cold, dark,
stupid cellar which I hate. We were there for
hours and hours. They kept pounding away. All
the neighbours were with us.

AGAIN! Again and again they keep sinking all our
boats, taking and dashing all our hopes. People
said that they wouldn't do it any more. That there
would soon be an end to it, that everything would
resolve itself. THAT THIS STUPID WAR
WOULD END!

Oh God, why do they spoil everything?
Sometimes I think it would be better if they kept
shooting, so that we wouldn't find it so hard
when it starts up again. This way, just as you relax,
it starts up AGAIN. I am convinced now that it
will never end. Because some people don't want
it to, some evil people who hate children and
ordinary folk.

I keep thinking that we're alone in this hell, that
nobody is thinking of us, nobody is offering us a
helping hand. But there are people who are
thinking and worrying about us.

Yesterday the Canadian TV crew and Janine came to see how we had survived the mad shelling. That was nice of them. Really kind.

And when we saw that Janine was holding an armful of food, we got so sad we cried. Alexandra came too.

People worry about us, they think about us, but sub-humans want to destroy us. Why? I keep asking myself, why? We haven't done anything. We're innocent. But helpless!

Zlata

Zlata Filipović (from Zlata's Diary)

Talk about your reading with a partner.

What impression of Zlata and her family and friends do you get from the diary?

How do the diary entries change as the civil war spreads?

What effect does reading the diaries have on you?

Write a letter to Zlata. Say what reading her diary made you think and feel.

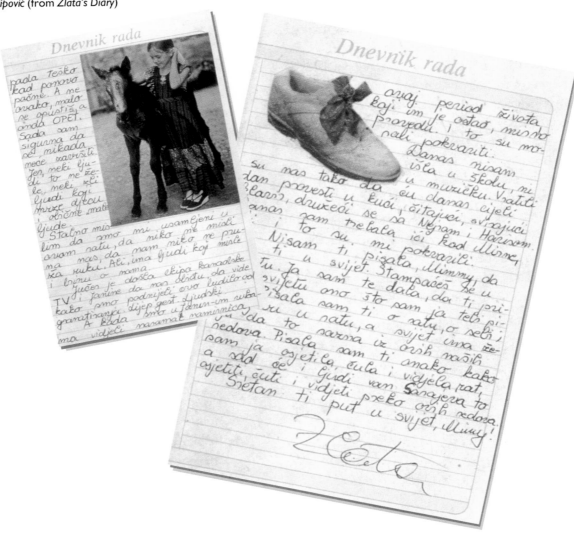

2 Writing as if you were there

How would *you* react in Zlata's situation? Could you record such frightening and dramatic events?

The extracts below are from another famous diary, written by a Dutch girl called Anne Frank. The diary describes her life in Amsterdam during the German occupation of Holland.

> Read the extracts. Like Zlata, Anne Frank wrote as if she were addressing her diary. She called her diary 'Kitty'.

A diary under occupation

Friday, 9th October, 1942

Dear Kitty,

I've only got dismal and depressing news for you today. Our many Jewish friends are being taken away by the dozen. These people are treated by the Gestapo without a shred of decency, being loaded into cattle trucks and sent to Westerbork, the big Jewish camp in Drente. Westerbork sounds terrible; only one washing cubicle for a hundred people and not nearly enough lavatories. There is no separate accommodation. Men, women, and children all sleep together. One hears of frightful immorality because of this; and a lot of the women, and even girls, who stay there any length of time are expecting babies.

It is impossible to escape; most of the people in the camp are branded as inmates by their shaven heads and many by their Jewish appearance.

If it is like this in Holland, whatever will it be like in the distant and barbarous regions they are sent to? We assume that most of them are murdered. The British radio speaks of their being gassed.

Perhaps that is the quickest way to die. I feel terribly upset. I couldn't tear myself away while Miep told these dreadful stories; and she herself was equally wound up for that matter. Just recently, for instance, a poor old crippled Jewess was sitting on her doorstep; she had been told to wait there by the Gestapo, who had gone to fetch a car to take her away. The poor old thing was terrified by the guns that were shooting at British planes overhead, and by the glaring beams of the searchlights. But Miep did not dare take her in; no one would undergo such a risk. The Germans strike without the slightest mercy. Elli too is very quiet: her boyfriend has got to go to Germany. She is afraid that the airmen who fly over our homes will drop their bombs, often weighing a million kilos, on Dirk's head. Jokes such as 'he's not likely to get a million' and 'it only takes one bomb' are in rather bad taste. Dirk is certainly not the only one who has to go; trainloads of boys leave daily. If they stop at a small station *en route*[1], sometimes some of them manage to get out unnoticed and escape; perhaps a few manage it. This, however, is not the end of my bad news. Have you ever heard of hostages? That's the latest thing in penalties for sabotage. Can you imagine anything so dreadful?

Prominent citizens – innocent people – are thrown into prison to await their fate. If the saboteur can't be traced, the Gestapo simply put

about five hostages against the wall. Announcements of their deaths appear in the papers frequently. These outrages are described as 'fatal accidents'. Nice people, the Germans! To think that I was once one of them too! No, Hitler took away our nationality long ago. In fact, Germans and Jews are the greatest enemies in the world.

Yours, Anne

Wednesday, 13th January, 1943
Dear Kitty,
Everything has upset me again this morning, so I wasn't able to finish a single thing properly.

It is terrible outside. Day and night more of those poor miserable people are being dragged off, with nothing but a rucksack and a little money. On the way they are deprived even of these possessions. Families are torn apart, the men, women and children all being separated. Children coming home from school find that their parents have disappeared. Women return from shopping to find their homes shut up and their families gone.

The Dutch people are anxious too, their sons are being sent to Germany. Everyone is afraid.

And every night hundreds of planes fly over Holland and go to German towns, where the earth is ploughed up by their bombs, and every hour hundreds and thousands of people are killed in Russia and Africa. No one is able to keep out of it, the whole globe is waging war and, although it is going better for the Allies, the end is not yet in sight.

And as for us, we are fortunate. Yes, we are luckier than millions of people. It is quiet and safe here, and we are even so selfish as to talk about 'after the war', brighten up at the thought of having new clothes and new shoes, whereas we really ought to save every penny, to help other people, and save what is left from the wreckage after the war.

The children here run about in just a thin blouse and clogs; no coat, no hat, no stockings, and no one helps them. Their tummies are empty, they chew an old carrot to stay the pangs, go from their cold homes out into the cold street and, when they get to school, find themselves in an even colder classroom. Yes, it has even got so bad in Holland that countless children stop the passers-by and beg for a piece of bread. I could go on for hours about all the suffering the war has brought, but then I would only make myself more dejected. There is nothing we can do but wait as calmly as we can till the misery comes to an end. Jews and Christians wait, the whole earth waits; and there are many who wait for death …

Yours, Anne

Anne Frank (from *The Diary of Anne Frank*)

With your partner, compare the two extracts. What different impressions do you get of Anne, her personality and the life she leads?

Write a brief description of her character as shown by these extracts.

Imagine that you and your family are living through a dramatic period in history. It could be a time of war, revolution or some natural or human disaster.

Write a series of entries from your diary.

'And as for us, we are fortunate.'
Anne's father was the only member of her family to survive. The others, including Anne, died in the concentration camps of Auschwitz and Belsen.

'The people are . . . being loaded into cattle trucks and sent to Westerbork . . .'
From Westerbork they were sent, in trains like this, to Auschwitz.

... on writing effective diary entries

 Diaries can take many forms, but they all have some features in common:

Diaries are personal

A diary records the events that the writer hears and sees. It is a personal record.

A diary also gives a writer the chance to react to events and to reflect on them. Diary entries record these reactions at the time when the entry was written.

 Diaries are a private form of writing

Diaries describe people by nicknames and talk about places as if the reader is familiar with them. The writing is conversational and chatty, as if the writer is talking to the pages in front of him or her.

 Diaries are detailed

A diary always includes details. The writer never knows what is going to seem important in later years when he or she re-reads the diary.

For example, a diary will record the first meeting with someone *as it happens*, not as the writer remembers it much later. Small details which seem trivial at the time can become interesting when you are re-reading a diary later.

 Diaries are authentic

A diary which is true will always read in a convincing way. If you describe events, provide details – some important and some trivial – and include your thoughts on these, you will produce a diary which rings true.

3 Writing your own diary

You are unlikely to be living in times that are as momentous as those described by Zlata or Anne. No doubt you are grateful for that! But your diary would still be interesting to somebody reading it in a hundred years' time. After all, you are growing up at the end of one century and looking forward to the next.

Keep a diary for the week ahead.
Write an entry for each day.

Follow these steps for success:

1 **Set aside a quiet time each day**
Just before you go to sleep is ideal. You will be relaxed and able to reflect on the whole day.

2 **Write about what happened during your day**
Try to include what you noticed or thought important. Mention family and friends where necessary, so that the picture of your world has real characters in it.

3 **Let your diary writing flow**
You are not writing your diary for anyone else. You only need to worry about redrafting and organising it if you are writing it for someone else to read.

4 **Keep the entries neat and legible**
Imagine looking back in years to come and not being able to read what you wrote!

5 **At the end of your week, prepare your diaries for publication**
You may want to keep your diary to yourself. That's fine.

If you *do* decide to show your diary to other people, you may have to make some changes to it. However, don't cut too much out or make too many changes or your diary won't feel authentic.

Explain who the people are that you mention in your diary and give a guide to any nicknames you use for them.

6 **Proof-read your diary**
Whether you are publishing your diary or not, check your spelling and punctuation and make sure that the final version is neat.

on target

After working through this unit, could you:

- describe the main features of diary writing to a friend?

- keep a more interesting diary of your next holiday?

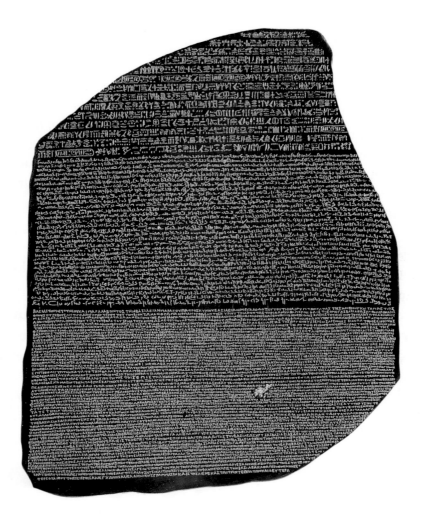

Early writing

When and where did writing begin? How did it develop, and how did our alphabet come into being?

In this unit you will explore how written language developed from speech. You will also investigate how early systems of writing worked.

The importance of speech

As humans we learn to speak before we can write. In the same way, the written version of a language always develops after the spoken version. There have been thousands of spoken languages, but only about one hundred of them have ever been put into writing.

The passage below, set in the seventeenth century, describes a meeting between the Algonkin Indians and Champlain, the leader of a French colony in Canada. The Algonkins had no written form of language. Instead, they recalled things from memory.

As the speech was translated, sentence by sentence, the assembly of Algonkins uttered the customary sounds of approval. Two leaders rose and squatted before him. One began to speak. In the traditional manner of the Algonkin, he first repeated what Champlain had said and then summarised what had been said on this subject on previous occasions. The Algonkin, having no written language, conducted all their affairs in this manner, constantly astonishing the French by their remarkable feats of recall.

Talk in a small group about what life would be like without writing.

What things would not exist?

What would school be like?

Would it be possible to live as we do?

Will television and video ever make writing unnecessary?

Report back to the class.

2 Using pictures in writing

The earliest writing dates from around 3500 BC. It was developed by the Sumerians and was in the form of *pictograms*. Pictograms were small pictures that communicated a meaning.

At first the pictures were drawn on clay with a sharp stick. These pictures were very realistic. They resembled the objects they stood for.

Gradually, the writers began to use a wedge-shaped stylus (an early form of pen), and the pictures became less realistic and more symbolic. This made the pictures harder to recognise, but it also meant that one Sumerian's writing was similar to another's.

THE DEVELOPMENT OF A PICTOGRAM
WHICH ORIGINALLY REFERRED TO A COW.

As the pictograms came to look less like objects, people began to use them in a more general way. For example, the sign for a foot could mean 'to walk', 'to stand up' or 'to move'. Each sign would be given a different sound and meaning depending on how it was used.

As a result, the Sumerians needed fewer written words. Over fifteen hundred of the early (realistic) pictograms have been identified, but only about six hundred of the later symbols.

These symbols, made up from wedge-shaped marks on clay, were known as *cuneiform*, from the Latin word *cuneus* (meaning 'wedge').

BIRD				
FISH				
DONKEY				
OX				
SUN				
GRAIN				

Use pictograms to write the following messages.

To a friend:

> I will meet you behind the cycle sheds after school with my old computer game. Bring the £5, and you can have it.

To your teacher:

> I was away from school yesterday because I cut my leg doing my paper round and had to go to hospital.
> I had three stitches, but I am fine today.

Compare your versions in groups. Which messages are the clearest, and why?

3 Adding sounds to writing

The Egyptians used a writing system based on signs, called *hieroglyphics*. This system dates back to 2900 BC. It died out around AD 390, but by then the number of signs had increased from 700 to almost 5000.

Hieroglyphic writing was the first language to represent some sounds by letters. The Egyptians used to carve it on temples and tombs, and there are many examples of this writing in Ancient Egyptian monuments.

Use the hieroglyphic alphabet printed on this page to write the name of a famous person. Ask a partner to work it out. The English and Egyptian systems do not match up precisely, so you may have to find an Egyptian sound to stand for an English letter.

a	b	c
vulture	foot	basket
d	e	f
hand	eye	horned snake
g	h	i
jar stand	wick	flowering reed
j	k	l
cobra	basket	resting lion
m	n	o
owl	water	quail chick
p	q	r
mat	hillside	mouth
s	t	u
folded cloth	loaf	quail chick and mouth
v	w	x
horned snake	quail chick	basket and folded cloth
y	z	
two reed leaves	door bolt	

4 Using an alphabet

The first *alphabet* appeared in Phoenicia around 1200 BC. An alphabet represents only sounds. In this it is unlike cuneiforms and hieroglyphics, where symbols can show either words or sounds.

The alphabet is divided into *vowels* (a, e, i, o, u) and *consonants* (all the other letters). The Phoenician alphabet only contained consonants. In learning to read individual words, students had to memorise the vowel sounds.

Aleph (à)	Beth (b)	Gimel (g)	Daleth (d)	He (h)	Vau (v)	Zayin (z)	Cheth (ch)	Teth (t)	Yod (y)	Kaph (k)
Lamed (l)	Mem (m)	Num (n)	Sameth (s)	Ayin (a)	Pe (p)	Tsade (ts)	Q'oph (q)	Resh (r)	Shin (sh)	Tau (t)

When the Greeks began using a Phoenician alphabet, around 800 BC, they added letters to show the vowel sounds that they used. They introduced the letters A (*alpha*), E(*epsilon*), O(*omega*) and Y (*upsilon*). I (*iota*) was added later. The Romans adapted the Greek alphabet. Our version comes from the Roman alphabet.

GREEK 500 B.C.	A	B	G	D	E	D	I	K	M	N	P	C	F	S	M	O	Q	R	L	X	T
ROMAN 500 B.C.	A	B	G	D	E	D	I	K	M	N	P	C	F	S	M	O	Q	R	L	X	T

> Make up a short message and write it out without any vowels, as the Phoenicians did. Swap your message with a partner and ask him or her to read it.
>
> Which words caused the most confusion? Why is this?

5 Using pictures again

We still use pictograms as a means of communication today. Pictograms are in daily use throughout the world in the form of signs, symbols, logos and computer icons.

With a partner, discuss why people might use a sign or symbol rather than write down their message.

Now design two of the following:

- a pictogram to mark an underground nuclear waste disposal site which will be dangerous for thousands of years

- a pictogram to be fixed to an unmanned space probe which will be sent to another galaxy

- a logo for a new organisation which plans to help homeless young people all over the world

- an icon for your computer which shows where your personal, and top secret, files are kept.

Display your designs and ask other people to interpret them. As a class, decide which work best, and why.

on target

After working through this unit, could you:

- give a short talk to another class on how writing developed?

- send a secret message to a friend?

- design a new traffic sign or an icon for a computer program?

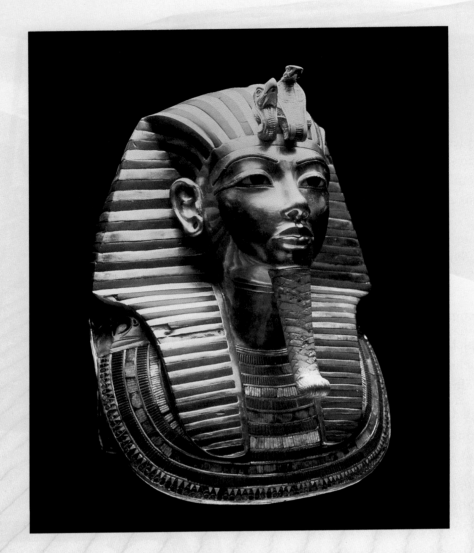

The tomb of the last Pharaoh

In this unit you will be taking part in an adventure. Your group will be searching for the lost tomb of Sarmion, the last of the Pharaohs of ancient Egypt.

 As you make your imaginary journey up the River Nile and across the desert, you will record what happens in different kinds of writing.

Making a start

The extract below is from the archeologist Howard Carter's account of the discovery of one of the most famous Egyptian tombs.

The day of days

The day following (26 November) was the day of days, the most wonderful that I have ever lived through, and certainly one whose like I can never hope to see again. Throughout the morning the work of clearing continued, slowly perforce, on account of the delicate objects that were mixed with the filling.

Then, in the middle of the afternoon, thirty feet down from the outer door, we came upon a second sealed doorway, almost an exact replica of the first. The seal impressions in this case were less distinct, but still recognisable as those of Tutankhamen and of the royal necropolis. Here again the signs of opening and re-closing were clearly marked upon the plaster. We were firmly convinced by this time that it was a cache that we were about to open, and not a tomb. The arrangement of stairway entrance passage and doors reminded us forcibly of the cache of Akhenaten and Tyi material found in the very near vicinity of the present excavation by Davis, and the fact that Tutankhamen's seals occurred there likewise seemed almost certain proof that we were right in our conjecture. We were soon to know. There lay the sealed doorway, and behind it was the answer to the question.

Slowly, desperately slowly it seemed to us as we watched, the remains of passage debris that encumbered the lower part of the doorway were removed, until at last we had the whole door clear before us. The decisive moment had arrived. With trembling hands I made a tiny breach in the upper left-hand corner. Darkness and blank space, as far as

an iron testing rod could reach, showed that whatever lay beyond was empty, and not filled like the passage we had just cleared. Candle tests were applied as a precaution against possible foul gases, and then, widening the hole a little, I inserted the candle and peered in, Lord Carnarvon, Lady Evelyn and Callender standing anxiously beside me to hear the verdict.

At first I could see nothing, the hot air escaping from the chamber causing the candle flame to flicker, but presently, as my eyes grew accustomed to the light, details of the room within emerged slowly from the mist, strange animals, statues, and gold – everywhere the glint of gold. For the moment – an eternity it must have seemed to the others standing by – I was struck dumb with amazement, and when Lord Carnarvon, unable to stand the suspense any longer, inquired anxiously, 'Can you see anything?' it was all I could do to get the words, 'Yes, wonderful things'. Then, widening the hole a little further, so that we both could see, we inserted an electric torch.

Howard Carter (from The Tomb of Tutankhamen)

As a group, discuss what you read on the previous page.

Do you know what was found in this tomb, and where it can now be seen?

Pick out three places where you can imagine exactly what Howard Carter saw, because the description is so detailed. Pick out two places where the feelings he experienced are described.

Look at the writing in detail. Make a list of the 'technical vocabulary', that is, the words to do with archaeology or Egyptian tombs. Use a dictionary to make sure you all understand the meaning of these words.

Now look at the length of the sentences. Are they all the same length? Which sentences put across the tension and excitement of the dicovery? The long, technical sentences? Or the short, simple sentences?

2 The quest begins

Your group's adventure is set in Egypt. Like Howard Carter's team, you are searching for a lost tomb.

Episode One the manuscript

First, give yourself an exciting or impressive name, like Indiana Jones, the hero of *Raiders of the Lost Ark*, or like Lady Evelyn in Carter's account. Talk about the kind of people you would like to be – an adventurer, a scientist, the cook,

a journalist. Note down the names of your fellow explorers so you can write about their exploits.

Start your journal by writing a brief description of yourself and of each member of the group.

Write your journal entry for the day when you discover the map that is going to lead you to the lost tomb. This is a day which begins normally but ends with excitement. Perhaps you find the map tucked inside an old book in a library or are given it by a frightened stranger in the street.

Draw the old map. It shows the ruined city of Tanis to the north on the banks of the River Nile. The river flows south, then divides into three tributaries. On the map are scribbled the following words:

Take the River that bleeds red and follow the Finger of Ra at the setting sun

Stick this map in your journal.

Episode Two | preparing to travel

You decide to leave for Egypt at once.

Below, are ten things you think it might be useful to include in your luggage. However, you haven't got that much space. With your team, decide on the five most important things to take with you. Remember to behave as your character would.

1 revolver with six bullets
2 nine metre long rope
3 compass
4 water bottle
5 two hand grenades
6 watch
7 flares for lighting or navigation
8 sheath knife
9 torch and spare battery
10 dehydrated food for six days

List in your journal the five items you are taking with you and the reasons why the team chose them. Say if you disagreed with any of the group's decision.

Episode Three | a journey by air and water

You fly to Cairo and hire an Arab dhow to sail you down the Nile to Tanis. The journey takes three days.

You are all glad to leave Cairo with its busy narrow streets. You are impressed by the ruins of Tanis, but sometimes you wish you could escape from the terrific heat, the flies, the new sounds, the new smells, the brilliant sunlit colours and the local food. On the dhow, the air is fresher and cooler.

Write a letter home to your family describing these three days. Capture the adventure and excitement, but also the uncertainty about the future. Your last paragraph should leave you sitting in your dhow looking out at the three streams that were shown on your map.

The tomb of the last Pharaoh

Episode Four   the stream that bleeds red

You know that you must sail up the stream that 'bleeds red', but what does this mean? Discuss what these words might possibly mean with your team.

You see a herdsman grazing his goats and ask for his advice, but even he seems to speak in riddles. This is what he says:

'The first stream is blessed by Allah, for it rises in the Mountains of the Moon and shines with the colour of a shark's belly.

'The middle stream tempts all forms of life and oozes liquid the colour of the heart of a pomegranate.

'The last springs from the heart of the desert and bleeds water the colour of a beautiful Ethiopian maiden.'

You travel up the middle stream, which soon becomes filled with a red weed that blocks your passage. Taking all your possessions, you leave the boat and follow the bank of the stream on foot. Hours later the stream becomes a trickle, and the trickle becomes sand. The sun has set and the stars have risen. A caravan of merchant traders passes by, and you buy a camel from them.

Your team is angry and tired. Some of you think that the decision to go up the middle river was a mistake. The camels were very expensive because the merchants realised you were in trouble. You are all very tired.

Improvise a scene that evening where tempers run high and disagreements between you come to a head. Act in character.

Episode Five across the desert sands

You travel for hours. The desert stretches out before you with no hint of anything that might be called the Finger of Ra.

Then you realise that you are no longer travelling on soft sand – the ground seems firmer. It is – it's grass! And in front of you a valley has opened up surrounded by the gentle curves of what look like green hills. You don't know where you are, but whatever it is it certainly isn't on any map.

The valley becomes steeper and steeper until you are forced to abandon your camel. You begin walking along the river bed of a towering canyon.

Write a description of this strange fertile canyon and the secret river.
Use adjectives and comparisons to convey its strange beauty.

Suddenly you stop. In front of you is a single column of eroded rock in the shape of a closed fist with a raised index finger. You all know immediately that this is the Finger of Ra!

However, you still have a puzzle to sort out. How can a finger of rock and the rising of the sun possibly show you the entrance to the tomb?

Discuss this problem with your team. Sunset is only fifteen minutes away!

Write a journal entry to explain the problem and your solution to it. Use diagrams if this helps. Remember to capture the tension of the situation as you see whether or not your idea works.

The tomb of the last Pharaoh

 Episode Six entering the tomb

You were right!

The following morning you enter the tomb and move into the darkness of the tunnel.

Your foot brushes a hidden wire, and a giant boulder drops behind you to block your exit. Now there is only one way out – forward.

You keep walking but become slightly worried when you hear scuttling noises and crunching sounds. Looking down, you see that the floor beneath and in front of you is covered in scorpions!

Write your story describing what happens as you journey down the corridor. Write in the first person and the present tense. Use short sentences to capture the tension of the journey.
For example:
'I am entering the tunnel. It's getting darker. Thank heavens I brought the torch!'

Suddenly, the corridor comes to an apparent dead end. Three fountains gurgle laughingly at you and you are about to drown your sorrows when, by the light of the torch, you notice faint markings on the wall above each fountain.

The first says, 'Drink deep and find everlasting contentment!'

The second says, 'Drink of my richness and find your destiny!'

The third says, 'Drink the bitter water of life and face eventual death!'

Decide which spring you think is safe to drink from.

There was a disagreement. One of your team chose the wrong fountain.

Write a short script of the scene which led up to this disaster. Show how you attempted to persuade him or her that you were right.

| Episode Seven | the Diamond of Ka

Stepping carefully through the secret doorway you enter the Tomb of Sarmion. Looking forward along the tunnel which now faces you, you are not quite sure, but there appears to be a slight gleam of light. Scrambling down the corridor you see that you are right.

You rush down the passageway, ploughing through the dirt and cobwebs, until you burst into an immense room. The light is coming from a tiny hole high above in the roof, and its triangular beam casts itself over the floor to reveal an amazing sight – the tomb of the last Pharaoh!

The room is about fifteen metres square, and, in the centre of the room, you see what you have always dreamt of – the sarcophagus of Sarmion. Standing at his head is the huge stone statue of a powerful warrior armed with a massive sword and, at his feet, you see something resting on a bronze pedestal.

Something gleaming brightly – the legendary Diamond of Ka!

You cannot believe in your good fortune. Kneeling by the pedestal at the foot of the warrior, you hold the diamond in your hand, tenderly brush away the dust and hold it up to the light.

At that instant two terrible things begin to happen. First of all, there is a dull rumbling deep within the mountain which shakes the ground beneath you. At the same time, the statue begins to come to life, striding aggressively and reaching out towards you. He raises his sword, and you realise that you must do battle with this stone creature.

How can you possibly win?

Write the story of how you and the remaining members of your team manage to overcome the statue, and how you escape from the collapsing chamber with the Diamond of Ka.

Perhaps the light pouring from the roof may help. Do you have any pieces of equipment in your rucksack which will help you now?

Afterword | fame and fortune

You are now a famous explorer. Everyone wants to hear your story.

Design and write a newspaper article about the horrors of the journey.

Look at the inside pages of a tabloid newspaper (one with small pages, like *Today* or the *Daily Mirror*) to help with your design.

Give your article a headline, use subheadings and leave space for pictures and maps.

Your article should cover two pages of the newspaper.

or

Write a letter to a film company. The company has shown interest in making a film of your ordeal, and you are replying.

Say what you think the main scenes would show and how one or two of the most exciting events could be portrayed.

on target

After working through this unit, could you:

- write a lively and detailed diary about events in your own life?

- make better decisions in co-operation with others?

Turned on its head

What makes a film or television comedy or a sketch funny?
One way is by showing something that is the opposite of what
the audience expects.

  In this unit you will be studying extracts from
two short plays. You will write a short script of
your own for presentation to the class.

1 Act out a scene

You probably all know something about the story of Robin Hood. Can you answer all these questions?

- Where did Robin live?
- Who was his main enemy, and what town did he come from?
- Who was the monk that helped him?
- What did Robin do with the money he stole?
- Who were the other members of his gang?

The extracts on these pages are from *Maid Marian and her Merry Men* by Tony Robinson. Working as a small group, prepare a reading of one of them for the class.

Extract 1
A meeting on the bridge

NARRATOR 1: Marian is about to cross the bridge. In front of her is a fierce man with an earring, a long thick staff and a big black beard. He is three feet tall.

LITTLE RON: There's no room on this bridge for the both of us. Stand aside stranger, or I, Little Ron, will knock you into the water.

MARIAN: Pardon?

LITTLE RON: See what a lusty staff I have, the very thing for cracking the pates of insolent rogues.

NARRATOR 2: Marian peers round the barrel she is carrying. She is seventeen, dumpy, with a wild shock of hair in which are little plaits with ribbons.

MARIAN: Look, I don't want to be rude, Mr Ron, but it's a very large bridge, and quite frankly you're not exactly massive, are you? I'm quite sure you could squeeze past if you wanted to.

LITTLE RON: We'll fight here on the bridge, so if one of us goes in the water, there'll be no doubt who has won, and the victor may go on their way without a wetting.

MARIAN: (*putting down the barrel*) And that's what you want?

LITTLE RON: Aye!

MARIAN: (*rolling up her sleeves*) We can't just sit down and talk about it?

LITTLE RON: Nay!

MARIAN: OK. Have it your way.

NARRATOR 2: Ron roars and swings at Marian. She ducks and he hurtles into the water.

MARIAN: (*peering over the edge of the bridge*) Are you all right?

NARRATOR 1: Ron stands in the water laughing like a maniac. He's been beaten but he's had a good fight.

Extract 2
Inventing the Merry Men

MARIAN: (*thoughtfully*) Robin. Robin! … Robin!!!

ROBIN: Are they coming?

MARIAN: No.

ROBIN: Have they gone?

MARIAN: Yes.

ROBIN: Then can I go home?

MARIAN: Home! Home! We've spent all morning clobbering Normans. You'll never be able to go home again.

NARRATOR 1: Robin's face slowly crumples. Is that a tear we see?

MARIAN: From now on, we'll have to live here in the forest.

ROBIN: What, buy a holiday cottage?

MARIAN: No Robin, we'll camp out under the stars.

ROBIN: But I haven't brought my wellingtons.

MARIAN: We'll make bows and arrows and we'll hold rich travellers to ransom.

ROBIN: (*suddenly interested*) Oh what, money d'you mean?

MARIAN: Yes, and we'll give it all to the poor.

ROBIN: I wanna go home!!!

NARRATOR 2: Marian leaps off into the middle of the glade. She is in the grip of a beautiful vision.

MARIAN: And we'll surround ourselves with a band of highly attractive, respectable young men who are just a *little* bit rough and … are dedicated to freeing our country from tyranny and injustice and … and … cruelty to animals and stuff … and we'll swing through the trees on long ropes, and we'll have our own costumes … and we'll never be cross or grumpy, and we'll do these fantastically brave deeds with a merry smile on our faces. And everyone will say 'Good heavens, it's those Merry Men, come in and have a cup of tea; can we have your autograph?' And no one will dare stand against us. And our names will go down in history, and we'll be famous forever and people will name pubs after us. What do you think?

ROBIN: (*pause*) We'll really have our own costumes?

MARIAN: Yes.

ROBIN: Originals, I mean, not out of a catalogue?

MARIAN: Yes.

ROBIN: Who's going to design them?

MARIAN: You?

ROBIN: (*pause*) Right – you're on. (*they shake hands excitedly*) I'll have to do some drawings, of course, but I think flared trousers, well, when I say flares, I don't mean, you know, 'flares', more a bit of fullness in the lower leg …

MARIAN: The clobber must wait till tomorrow, Robin. First, we must go to the aid of a tadpole in distress. Forward to Nottingham Castle.

Tony Robinson (from *Maid Marian and her Merry Men*)

2 What makes a scene funny?

Audiences laugh at plays for many different reasons. They might laugh at the way the actors look and behave, their *timing* (the way they say their lines at just the right moment), the reactions other actors have to them, or just because what happens is surprising or amusing.

One of the things that makes *Maid Marian and her Merry Men* funny is that it reverses the audience's expectations. In other words, it shows characters and events that are the opposite of those you would expect.

Working with a partner, explore how this happens. Look at:

- the names of the characters

- the events which take place

- things people do and say.

Use a chart like the one below to help you do this.

	What there is in the play	What you would expect
Names		
Events		
What people do		
What people say		

3 Reading
Bill's New Frock

Read the extracts on these pages from
Bill's New Frock by Anne Fine.

In this play, Bill, a boy, has turned into a girl
for the day. The play looks at what happens to
him and how he is treated by other people.

A school day with a difference

OLD LADY: Give me your hand, dear. Let me help you safely across the road.

BILL: No thanks. Don't drag me. Let go.

OLD LADY: There we are. Safe and sound.

BILL: I've crossed here every day for months and she's never done that before. It must be this awful pink frock.

MALCOLM: (*wolf-whistling*) Wheeeet-whooooo!

BILL: It is! It's this awful pink frock! Even Mean Malcolm doesn't know who I am. He's wolf-whistling at me. Yuk! Uh-uh. There's the Headmaster, and I'm late. I'd better get through the gates.

HEADMASTER: (*yelling*) Come along, you lads! Get your skates on! Move, David Irwin! Hurry along, Tom Warren! Stop dawdling, Andrew!

BILL: I'll just try and creep past …

HEADMASTER: (*sweetly*) That's right, dear. Come along. We wouldn't like to be late for school now, would we?

BILL: Is he talking to *me*? He's never spoken to me like that before. It must be the frock. At least it keeps you out of trouble.

BOY 1: Hey, you!

BILL: Whoops! Maybe it doesn't.

BOY 1: Hey, you! Aren't you listening? Get out of the way of our football game.

BILL: Football! Oh, great! I'll be on your side. OK. Here we go. Ready. Kick it this way!

BOY 2: Get out of the way, can't you?

BILL: But I'm playing football with you.

BOY 3: No, you're not.

BOY 1: You can't. Not in that frock. No one plays football in a fancy frock like that!

BILL: I do.

BOY 2: Don't be silly. You're holding up our game. Get out of the way!

BOY 3: Go and play in the girl's bit of the playground.

BILL: Oh, yes? And where's that?

BOY 3: (*pointing one way*) Over there.

BILL: There are boys playing football over there.

BOY 2: (*pointing the other way*) Over there, then.

BILL: There are more boys playing football over there.

BOY 1: Over here, then.

BILL: You're playing here. You're playing everywhere.

BOY 3: It's not *our* problem, is it? Just get out of the way, please. You're spoiling the game.

BILL: No wonder most of the girls end up stuck against the railings if they're not playing football! There's nowhere else for them to go. If they come out into the middle of the playground, they'll get run over –

BOY 1: ⎫
BOY 2: ⎬ Get out of the way!
BOY 3: ⎭

BILL: – just like I'm getting run over! Help!

(*The bell rings. Everyone runs off, leaving Bill like an upturned crab in the middle of the playground.*)

MRS COLLINS: Good morning, everybody.

WHOLE CLASS: Good-mor-ning-Mis-sus-Col-lins.

MRS COLLINS: And here's the Headmaster to speak to you.

HEADMASTER: Good morning, 4C.

WHOLE CLASS: Good-morning-Mis-ter-Phil-lips.

HEADMASTER: Now I want four strong volunteers to carry tables over to the playground for me.

ASTRID: Me, Sir!

BILL: Me, Sir!

KIRSTY: Me, Sir!

ROHAN: Me, Sir!

WHOLE CLASS: Me, Sir! I'm strong!

HEADMASTER: Right. This boy.

ROHAN: Yes , Sir.

HEADMASTER: And that boy.

MARTIN: Yes , Sir.

HEADMASTER: And that boy.

PHILIP: Yes, Sir.

HEADMASTER: And this boy.

ARIF: Yes, Sir.

HEADMASTER: Right. Off we go.

(*Four boys and Headmaster troop out*)

ASTRID: It's not fair, Mrs Collins.

FLORA: He always picks the boys to carry things.

MRS COLLINS: Perhaps the tables are heavy.

KIRSTY: None of the tables in this school are heavy.

ASTRID: And I know for a fact that I am stronger than at least three of the boys he picked.

BILL: It's true. Whenever we have a tug of war, everyone wants Astrid on their team.

MRS COLLINS: Oh, well. It doesn't matter. No need to make such a fuss. It's only a silly old table.

ALL THE GIRLS: But it *does* matter. To *us*.

MRS COLLINS: That's enough! Now everyone open your workbooks.

WHOLE CLASS: … mutter … mutter … mutter …

MRS COLLINS: And get on with your work. I'll come round and look at everyone's books in turn. You're first. What page are you doing?

BILL: This one.

MRS COLLINS: This is very messy. Look at this dirty smudge. And this one. And the edge of your book looks as if it's been *chewed*.

BILL: But I'm doing my best. And it's a lot better than what I did yesterday. Or the day before. In fact, it's a really good page – for me.

MRS COLLINS: Well it's not good enough for *me*. Now what about yours, Philip?

PHILIP: I'm doing this page.

MRS COLLINS: Not bad at all, Philip. Keep up the good work.

BILL: Let me see that, Philip.

PHILIP: Here you are.

BILL: But that's awful. That's disgusting. It's much, much worse than mine!

FLORA: Philip's letters are all wobbly.

TALILAH: They're straggling all over the page like camels lost in the desert.

BILL: It's much, much worse than mine. And she didn't say anything nice to me.

TALILAH: Or me.

FLORA: Or me.

PHILIP: Well, girls are *supposed* to be neater, aren't they?

ALL THE GIRLS: Why?

PHILIP: I don't know. They just *are*.

Anne Fine (from *Bill's New Frock*)

Answer these questions, using quotations from the extracts to back up what you say:

- How is Bill treated by Malcolm, the headteacher and Mrs Collins?
- How is this different from the way he is normally treated?
- What does Bill think about what is happening to him?
- What do the extracts tell you about the different ways in which girls and boys are treated?
- Is this how girls and boys are treated in *your* school?

4 Write your own script

Write your own short scene where the characters or events are turned on their head!

Imagine that the scene is part of a play intended for performance in the classroom. Follow these steps for success.

1 Think of a plot

You need a good idea to get started. Think about:

- Taking a well-known story and reversing what happens in it, for example:

  Binderella – the story of a beautiful princess who turns into a tramp

  Strange Hill– the school where the teachers cause trouble

- Making someone's life change in a dream. They could suddenly change sex or appearance, or take on a different personality. For example:

  Batwimp – the superhero who hates fighting

  Aikido Annie – the quiet girl who came back from holiday in China...

- Making something different happen in your play from what your audience expects to happen.

  Gerald, the friendly bank robber

  Bodgers – the shop that hates to serve you

2 Start with a plan

Decide what is going to happen in the scene you are about to write.

Note down who the characters are.

Keep your scene simple, so that it can be acted out for your class. Remember that a scene from a play takes place in the same amount of time as it would in life and that it has to be set in one place.

A bad plan:
Batwimp takes on invaders from space but has to come home to change his tights so the colour matches his spaceship.

A good plan:
One lunchtime, Batwimp comes to school to take on the bully in Year 11.

3 Write your script

To help you do this, imagine the scene in your head. Think of the words people would say and make your characters react to one another and to what happens.

Mrs Crump:	Annie, may I have a word with you?
Aikido Annie:	(*taking up a defensive karate position*) Ah, so!
Mrs Crump:	Stand still when I'm talking to you. Why is Wayne Smith lying on the floor in the hall clutching his stomach?
Aikido Annie:	Um …
Mrs Crump:	He says you kicked him hard in a sensitive place.

Aikido Annie:	(*indignant*) It wasn't a *kick*. It was a high-toed samosa with body swerve for maximum impact. You can make holes in walls with them.
Mrs Crump:	Does this episode have anything to do with the three tables in the dining room which appear to have snapped in half?

4 Redraft

One of the best ways to check your script is to read it with a partner. That should show you lines which are clumsy to say or which do not follow on from what was said before.

Be prepared to make changes.

5 Revise

It is important to check the script carefully for errors.

Make sure you have given enough advice about how things should be said and that you have set the scene out properly.

6 Proof-read and write the final version

Make a final check for errors. Watch out for punctuation errors as you write what characters say.

Keep the final version neat – other people will have to be able to read and follow your instructions.

... on how to set out a script on the page

> Number the scene and describe the setting.

Scene 2

The classroom at lunchtime. There are tables and chairs at odd angles. There are sandwich boxes, flasks and wrapping paper on the tables, as if several people have just had their lunch. Floyd, Shane and Jenny come into the classroom.

> Put the speakers' names in capital letters (or small capitals, as here) followed by a colon (:).

> Put instructions to the actors in brackets.

FLOYD: (*speaking as he walks in*) That Annie's gone nuts. Did you see what she did to Wayne?

SHANE: What happened? Someone said she just took off her glasses and whizzed straight at him. That's not like Dripfeed.

JENNY: Yeah, I bet you wouldn't call her that to her face now. That Wayne deserved it though.

FLOYD: Hey, Shane! (*Shane turns*) I dare you. Call her Dripfeed again at registration!

> Try to reflect how people speak, but make sure that what you write is well punctuated. If it's not, it will be confusing to read.

> Make your characters react to what they hear.

5 Perform your script

Working in a group, read each other's scripts through together.

Choose one scene to act out for the rest of the class to watch.

 **on target**

After working through this unit, could you:

- describe what makes a comic sketch funny?

- write and set out a playscript?

- give a group of friends advice on improving their own play?

Getting into print

We spend a lot of our time reading, but how often do we stop and think about the way words and pictures are arranged on the page?

 In this unit you will explore how different kinds of print affect the way we read. You will also learn about typefaces (fonts), point size and other aspects of layout.

abcdefghijklmnopqrstuvwxyz

1 Choosing a typeface

Each person has a different way of forming the individual letters that make up words. In other words, we all have different styles of handwriting.

The same is true about print. Typewriters normally have only one way of forming letters, but there are actually hundreds of different ways of doing this.

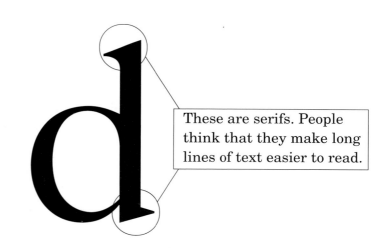

These are serifs. People think that they make long lines of text easier to read.

We call these different ways of forming printed letters *typefaces*. Typefaces come in three different forms: *serif*, *sans serif* and *decorative*. The different typefaces based on these are called *fonts*.

The letters in this sentence use a serif font.

The letters in this sentence use a sans serif font.

The letters in this sentence use a decorative font.

A *serif* is the small addition to the end of a stroke of a letter. Fonts that do not use them are called *sans serif* (from the French word *sans* meaning 'without').

a b c d e f g h i j k l m n o p q r s t u v w x y z

Make a chart like the one below. Look at the various pieces of text on this page. Place each example of text under the correct heading.

Words	serif	sans serif	decorative
City			
Free			
Letters			
Animal			
The vision			
It fits			
Ecologic			

Now, look at a wider range of written materials. Look at books, magazines and newspapers.

Try to answer the following questions:

- Which sort of typeface is the most common?

- Where did you find most serif fonts?

- Where do you find decorative fonts?

- What kind of books use sans serif fonts?

Share your findings with others in the group.

From what you have found out, draw up a set of rules to show when you should use a particular kind of font.

a b c d e f g h i j k l m n o p q r s t u v w x y z

2 Deciding on a size

Another thing that affects the way we read is the size of the print. Type is measured in *points*. A point is about 1/72 of an inch so that a letter in 72 point should be about one inch high.

I Read the following story.

8pt
Alice was beginning to get very tired of sitting by her sister on the bank, and of having nothing to do: once or twice she peeped into the book her sister was reading, but it had no pictures or conversations in it, 'and what is the use of a book,' thought Alice, 'without pictures or conversation?'

10pt
So she was considering in her own mind (as well as she could, for the hot day made her feel very sleepy and stupid), whether the pleasure of making a daisy chain would be worth the trouble of getting up and picking the daisies, when suddenly a White Rabbit, with pink eyes, ran close by her.

12pt
There was nothing so *very* remarkable in that; nor did Alice think it so *very* much out of the way to hear the Rabbit say to itself, 'Oh dear! Oh dear! I shall be too late!' (when she thought it over afterwards, it occurred to her that she ought to have wondered at this, but at the time it all seemed quite natural); but when the Rabbit actually *took a watch out of*

14pt
its waistcoat-pocket and looked at it, and then hurried on, Alice started to her feet, for it flashed across her mind that she had never before seen a rabbit with either a waistcoat-pocket, or a watch to take out of it, and, burning with curiosity, she ran across the field after it, and fortunately was just in time to see it pop down a large rabbit-hole under the hedge.

16pt
In another moment down went Alice after it, never once considering how in the world she was to get out again.

22pt
The rabbit-hole went straight on like a tunnel for some way, and then dipped suddenly down, so suddenly that Alice had not a moment to think about stopping herself before she found herself falling down a very deep well.

a b c d e f g h i j k l m n o p q r s t u v w x y z

Working with a partner, look back at the previous page and decide:

- which point size(s) you find easiest to read

- which point size(s) you think would not be suitable for use in your school textbooks

- where you might expect to find 8 point text

- where you might usually find the larger point sizes.

Report your findings back to the class. See whether or not you agree.

3 Using font and size for effect

Study the two newsletters presented below. The words are identical in each newsletter, and both were produced using the same computer program.

Compare the newsletters. Describe the differences between them.

Which one would you be most likely to pick up and read? Give your reasons.

As you write, think about the use of:

typefaces	boxes
columns	artwork
space	colour.

a b c d e f g h i j k l m n o p q r s t u v w x y z

Other writers use fonts and point sizes to express ideas. Read the following poem:

The Mouse's Tail

Fury said to
  a mouse, That
      he met
        in the
          house,
          'Let us
        both go
        to law:
      I will
    prosecute
    you.—
    Come, I'll
    take no
      denial;
        We must
            have a
              trial:
                For
                really
                this
                morning
                  I've
                nothing
                to do.'
            Said the
          mouse to
          the cur,
          'Such a
            trial,
          dear sir,
          With no
        jury or
        judge,
        would be
        wasting
          our breath.'
            'I'll be
            judge,
            I'll be
          jury,'
          said
            cunning
            old Fury;
              "I'll try
                the whole
                  cause,
                  and
                  condemn
                  you
                  to
                  death.'

Lewis Carroll

Why has Lewis Carroll made the words of the mouse's tale grow smaller?

Write your own poem that uses different fonts and point sizes.

At the planning stage, write neatly and pay attention to the size of the letters you use. Then, as you draft and work towards your final version, use a word-processing (WP) or desk-top publishing (DTP) program that allows you to change font sizes.

Here are some ideas to get your poem started:

- a whale or a shark coming closer to a ship
- a car skidding
- a parachute jump
- a vulture circling
- a lost satellite disappearing into space.

a b c d e f g h i j k l m n o p q r s t u v w x y z

... on ten things you should remember when starting desk-top publishing

1 Do not:

- forget about your readers
- use too many typefaces
- include too many special effects
- leave too little white space – the document will look cramped
- forget to use subheadings
- forget to proof-read
- use too many small illustrations.

2 Do:

- plan the document before you start
- choose your typeface carefully. Decorative fonts look nice, but they are hard to read.
- use paragraphs. Short passages of text are easier to read than long ones.

4 Design your own newsletter

You are now going to write and design your own newsletter.

Follow these six steps for success:

1 Make a sketch of your planned layout
Decide on whether to use columns and, if so, how many.

2 Select the typeface
You need to decide on the style for your headlines, subheadings and the main part of the writing.

3 Think about pictures and any 'special effects' you will use

4 Start writing the stories that will fill your newsletter

5 Make a 'mock-up' of your design
Cut up newspapers or magazines, arrange headlines, stories and pictures on the page and then paste them down.

6 Write out the stories for your newsletter in the column widths you have decided
If you are writing the newsletter by hand, make sure your own handwriting is as neat as possible.

If you are using a WP or a DTP program you may be able to do all your work on screen. If not, print out your stories in columns and then cut and paste them on to a sheet of paper.

a b c d e f g h i j k l m n o p q r s t u v w x y z

5 Publishing your newsletter

Having produced your newsletter, you can now distribute it.

If your work has been prepared on computer, you can print out several copies. If you have used handwriting, you may be able to make some photocopies.

> In groups, discuss the newsletters that the class has produced.
>
> Suggest changes that might have improved the newsletters.
>
> Decide which newsletters are best. Give your reasons.

on target

After working through this unit, could you:

- choose the right typeface for the right job?

- advise a group of people who were planning a newsletter?

- comment on the use made of typefaces in your favourite magazine?

a b c d e f g h i j k l m n o p q r s t u v w x y z

Glossary

The words listed here all appear in this book and are all used in English lessons.

This glossary helps you to understand what these words mean and gives you an idea of how you can use them. All the examples from poetry are taken from *The Rime of the Ancient Mariner* by Samuel Taylor Coleridge, unless it says otherwise.

The word		What it means
accent	=	the way in which words are pronounced. Accents change from region to region, but the introduction of travel and television means that the differences between them are becoming less obvious. All languages are spoken in a variety of accents.
adjective	=	the describing words which modify the meaning of nouns. An adjective usually (but not always) goes in front of a noun in English. 'The *thick black* cloud was cleft, and still The moon was at its side: Like waters shot from some *high* crag, The lightning fell with never a jag, A river *steep* and *wide*.'
alliteration	=	repeating the same first letter in a series of words. Alliteration is mostly used in poetry, but you will find examples in headlines, advertisements and slogans. 'The *fair* breeze blew, the white *foam flew*, The *furrow followed free*,'
assonance	=	repeating the same vowel sounds in a series of words. Assonance is mostly used in poetry, but it is also to be found in nursery rhymes, television commercials and persuasive talk. 'The ice was here, the ice was there, The ice was all around; *It cracked and growled, and roared and howled,* Like noises in a swound.'
audience	=	the people who listen to what you say or read your writing. Your audience may be people you know, but they may also be people you do not know. You have to think about who your audience will be as you plan what you want to say.
author	=	how you refer to the writer of a story, play or poem when you are writing about or discussing your reading.
character	=	a person in a story or play.
clause	=	a group of words that contain a verb and make sense on their own. '*At first it seemed a little speck,* And then it seemed a mist:'

The word		What it means
conclusion	=	the ending of a piece of writing or a talk. A good conclusion makes talks and writing more interesting by summing up what has gone before.
consonant	=	any letter in the alphabet that is not a vowel. There are twenty-one consonants and five vowels in our alphabet. You will find a consonant sound at the beginning or end of most words.
conversational	=	a way of describing a style of talk or writing that is chatty – as if it was taking place between friends. It is used in stories and in writing designed to help a reader – for example, a children's book or a leaflet giving advice.
description	=	using words to show what something or someone is like. Description is also used to talk and write about *how* writing is effective.
dialect	=	a different variety of the language of a country. A dialect has its own words (vocabulary), word order and grammar. It is often connected with one particular region. In English, many regional dialects are used in speech, but most writing uses standard English. As with accents, the differences in dialects are becoming less obvious.
direct speech	=	using the actual words people say in stories in order to make them more realistic. Direct speech is usually placed within speech marks.
		'Make sure that you use a capital letter at the start of each section of direct speech, a punctuation mark at the end and that you begin a new line for each new speaker,' said Mr Holmes.
		'Make sure you read my story,' whispered Kevin, 'instead of just covering it in red ink.'
draft	=	the first – rough – version of a piece of writing. A draft is sometimes written as notes or a plan.
dramatise	=	turning a story or poem into a scene from a play. There are often dramatisations of well-known novels on television.
first person	=	writing a story using 'I', as if you were really in the events you are describing. The first person can bring a story to life or make a speech sound more heartfelt and convincing. It is almost always used in autobiography, where you write about yourself.
formal letters	=	letters you write to people you do not know. Formal letters include applications for jobs and letters to magazines and newspapers in which you give your opinions. You set out names and addresses on formal letters in a conventional way and you write these letters in standard English.
icon	=	a small picture or diagram used regularly as a visual reminder for something.
image	=	a picture in words, or the mixture of pictures and words, that make up an advertisement or a scene from a film. You also use the word 'image' to describe the overall impression given by a film or groups of people.
improvise	=	making up a play scene on a particular subject or theme 'as you go along'. Most improvisations are done in groups.
layout	=	the arrangement of words, or words and pictures, on a page. You talk about layout mostly when you are writing about posters, magazines and leaflets or experimenting with desktop publishing.

Glossary

The word		What it means
logo	=	the icon used by a company to link its products together. A logo is a visual symbol chosen by a company (or another organisation) to represent its image.
metaphor	=	a form of comparison that is often used in poetry or descriptive writing. Metaphors compare two things without using words such as 'like' or 'as'. They generally add to the effect of the writing.
		'Thou art the ruins of the noblest man That ever lived in the tide of times.' (*Julius Caesar*)
mime	=	a play or scene without words, where all the meaning is shown by action and gesture.
narrator	=	the person who tells the story in a novel or short story. A narrator can be the writer but may also be a character in the story.
nouns	=	words which name objects, places and things. *Abstract nouns* name qualities like 'evil' or 'generosity'.
onomatopoeia	=	the use of words – like 'bang', 'woof', 'cuckoo' – where the sound helps you think of the meaning. Onomatopoeia is often used in poems for effect:
		'Yea, *slimy* things did crawl with legs Upon the *slimy* sea.' 'And every soul it passed me by Like the *whizz* of my cross-bow!'
paragraph	=	a group of sentences that are linked together by their meaning. Paragraphs usually start with their first word set in slightly from the margin. Otherwise there is often a blank line between paragraphs.
personification	=	a form of comparison where a thing is described as if it is human or alive. Personification is often used in poetry or talk:
		'And now the storm-blast came and *he* was tyrannous and strong: *He* struck with *his* o'ertaking wings, And *chased* us south along.'
phrase	=	a group of words that are connected but do not make sense on their own:
		'And every tongue, *through utter drought,* Was withered at the root; We could not speak, no more than if We had been choked with soot.'
plot	=	the main events in a story. The plot of a story is often used to summarise that story.
present tense	=	writing about things as if they are taking place at the present time. The present tense is used for descriptions and in factual writing.
purpose	=	the reason why you are writing, or talking. Understanding what your purpose is helps you to shape your writing and make decisions about length and the level of vocabulary to use.

The word		What it means
rhyme	=	the linking of sounds at the end of lines in poetry. Rhyme creates a sense of movement. It is also used in songs, children's games and advertising. The *rhyme scheme* of a poem describes which lines rhyme with one another and shows where new rhymes start.
rhythm	=	the regular beat of the words in poetry or rhyme. Rhythm is created by the patterns of sounds in a word.
scene	=	part of a play set in one place and at one time. A new scene starts when either the time or the place alters.
sentence	=	a group of words which make sense when written on their own. Sentences begin with a capital letter and end with a full stop, a question mark or an exclamation mark.
simile	=	a very common form of comparison which uses the words 'like' or 'as':

'Day after day, day after day,
We stuck, no breath nor motion;
As idle as a painted ship
Upon a painted ocean.'

standard English	=	the dialect of English that is accepted as the correct form for writing. People who speak a regional dialect at home often speak standard English in formal situations.
style	=	a way of describing the collected features of a piece of writing – the choice of words, the length of sentences, the use of direct speech or specialist language. The style of a piece of writing can be formal or informal, old-fashioned or modern, detailed and descriptive, or bare.
theme	=	an idea, a belief or a moral that runs through a story, play or poem.
typeface	=	the shape of the letters used in print. The typefaces used by word processors are known as 'fonts'.
verbs	=	words that describe actions. Verbs are modified by adverbs (most of which end in '-ly'), just as nouns are modified by adjectives. The verbs in the lines below are in *italics*; the adverbs are in **bold**:

'**Swiftly, swiftly** *flew* the ship,
Yet she *sailed* **softly** too:
Sweetly, sweetly *blew* the breeze –
On me alone it *blew*.'

vocabulary	=	the choice of the words used in talking or writing. Your audience (those you are writing to) and your purpose (why you are writing) will influence your vocabulary. Depending on your audience and purpose, your vocabulary will be simple or complex, expert or non-expert, extensive or limited.
vowels	=	the letters a, e, i, o ,u. Vowels make more than five sounds because they can be combined in words.

Acknowledgements

We are grateful to the following for permission to reproduce copyright material:

the author, Valerie Bloom, for her poem 'Haircut'; Faber & Faber Ltd for the poem 'Valentine' by Wendy Cope from **Serious Concerns** and the poem 'My Heart' by Vikram Seth from **All You Who Sleep Tonight** (1990); the author's agent, for an extract from **Bill's New Frock** (Longman Hit Play Version) by Anne Fine, originally published by Methuen Children's Books; the author, Katherine Gallagher, for her poem 'Wheels-Song' from **Through a Window**, anthology edited by Wendy Body (Longman Book Project) and 'A Girl's Head' from **Fish-rings on Water**, published by Forest Books; Hachette Jeunesse for extracts from 'The Four Creations', 'The Rainbow Serpent' and 'Muluku and the Monkey Men' from **The Creation of the World** translated by Frances Halton, published by The Cherrytree Press Ltd; Harcourt Brace & Co. for the poem 'Phizzog' by Carl Sandberg from **Good Morning, America**, copyright 1928 and renewed 1956 by Carl Sandburg; Harper Collins for an extract from 'The Fellowship of the Ring' in **Lord of the Rings Part 1** by J.R.R. Tolkien; **Here's Health** for extracts from the articles 'It's 1pm and 12 year old James', 'Class of Junkies' and 'The road to illness . . .' by Sue Platt in **Here's Health**, March 1993; the author's agents on behalf of the Estate of the late Erich Kästner for an extract from **The Little Man** by Erich Kästner, published by Jonathan Cape Ltd; Longman Group Ltd for the story 'The Cow and the Giant' by Geraldine McCaughrean from **On the Day the World Began** (Longman Book Project); the author, Michaela Morgan, for her poem 'I don't cry' from **Through a Window**, anthology edited by Wendy Body (Longman Book Project); Orion Children's Books for an extract from **The Borrowers Afloat** by Mary Norton; Pavillion Books for an extract from **In the Beginning** by Virginia Hamilton; Penguin Books Ltd for an extract from **Zlata's Diary** by Zlata Filipović translated by Christina Pribichevich-Zorić (Viking 1994). Copyright © Fixot et éditions Robert Laffont, 1993, 'The Boy's Head' by Miroslav Holub from **Selected Poems**, translated by Ian Milner and George Theiner (Penguin Books 1967). Copyright © Miroslav Holub, 1967, translation copyright © Penguin Books Ltd, 1967; Penguin Books/Alfred A. Knopf Inc for the poem 'Upon Shaving Off One's Beard' by John Updike from **Tossing and Turning**, copyright © 1977 by John Updike, reprinted by permission, originally appeared in 'The New Yorker'; Raving Beauties for the poem 'Her Belly' by Anna Swirsczynska from **No Holds Barred** edited by the Raving Beauties, first published by The Women's Press Ltd, 1985, 34 Great Sutton Street, London ECIV ODX; the authors' agents for a sketch by Tony Robinson from **Maid Marian and Her Merry Men** (Longman Hit Plays); Transworld Publishers Ltd for an extract from **Truckers** by Terry Pratchett; Vallentine Mitchell & Co Ltd for an extract from **The Diary of Anne Frank** by Anne Frank; The Watts Publishing Group for the poem 'My Dad' by Julie O'Callaghan from **Taking my Pen for a Walk**.

We are grateful to the following for permission to reproduce photographs:

AFF/AFS — Amsterdam the Netherlands pages 97 (top), 97 (bottom) and 99 (top); Bildarchiv Preußische Kultur Besitz/Berlin page 99 (bottom); Ancient Art & Architecture Collection, page 102, page 104, page 108 (Ronald Sheridan); BBC page 121; The Bridgeman Art Library page 50 (top);

Sandy Brownjohn page 129; Calm Feelings page 118; Julian Cotton page 45; Dagnino/Cosmos/Impact page 33 (centre right); Eye Ubiquitous pages 21, 33 (centre) (Davy Bold), 33 (centre bottom), 33 (centre left) (L Fordyce), 87 (L Fordyce), 107 (upper centre left) (Paul Seheult), 107 (lower centre left) (Paul Seheult), 107 (lower centre right) (Paul Thompson), 112 (Mike Southern); Hulton-Deutsch Collection pages 14 (right), 30, 41, 42, 51 (centre left) and 78; The Image Bank pages 33 (top) (Infocus International), 33 (top right) (Werner Bokelberg), 33 (bottom left) (Michael Friedel), 50 (bottom) (G M Covian), 107 (upper centre right) (Eddie Hironaka), 112 (inset) (François Dardelet); The Kobal Collection pages 14 (centre), 50 (centre) and 117; Life File page 51 (centre right) (Keith Duncan); Magnum Photos pages 90, 93 and 94 (all Paul Lowe/Magnum); Mary Evans Picture Library pages 56 and 109; Redferns page 15; Rex Features pages 51 (top) and 93 (top) (© Alexandra Boulat); Science Photo Library page 31 (David Parker); Andrew Steeds page 137; Tony Stone Worldwide, pages 22–3, 24–5, page 51 (bottom) (Alain le Garsmeur), page 135 (Dan Smith); Zefa UK Ltd pages 16 (bottom left), 18, 19 and 28; John Walmsley page 103.

We would also like to thank the following for help in the production of this book: The staff and pupils of Oxted County School, Oxted.

Every effort has been made to trace and acknowledge ownership of copyright. The publishers will be glad to make suitable arrangements with any copyright holders whom it has not been possible to contact.

LONGMAN GROUP LIMITED

Longman House, Burnt Mill, Harlow, Essex CM20 2JE, England and Associated Companies throughout the world.

First published 1995
ISBN 0 582 23982 6

Designed by Pentacor PLC (*Warren Kerley*)

Illustrations by Rowan Barnes Murphy, Duncan Burrow, Phil Dobson, Trevor Dunton, Paul Hess, Warren Kerley, Vicky Lowe, Colin Smithson, John Smyth.

Set in 11 pt, New Century Schoolbook, Linotron 300
Produced by Longman Singapore Publishers (Pte) Ltd.
Printed in Singapore.